THERESIENSTADT
Survival in Hell

Theresienstadt
Survival in Hell

MÉLANIE OPPENHEJM

Translated by
DINA ULLENDORFF

Foreword by
EDWARD ULLENDORFF

Preface by
RALPH OPPENHEJM

2001

MENARD PRESS
in association with the
European Jewish Publication Society
ejps

First published in Great Britain in 2001
by Menard Press in association with the
European Jewish Publication Society, EJPS
PO Box 19948, London N3 3XJ
Website : www.ejps.org.uk

Worldwide distribution (except North America)
Central Books/Troika
99 Wallis Road, Hackney Wick, London E9 5LN
Telephone 020 8986 4854   *Fax* 020 8533 5821

Distribution in North America
Small Press Distribution Inc.
1341 Seventh Street, Berkeley, CA 94710, USA

ISBN 1 874320 28 4

The Menard Press
8 The Oaks, Woodside Avenue
London N12 8AR, UK
Telephone and fax 020 8446 5571

Typeset by Antony Gray
Printed and bound in Great Britain by
Alden Press, Oxford

The European Jewish Publication Society is a
registered charity which gives grants to assist
in the publication and distribution of books
relevant to Jewish literature, history,
religion, philosophy, politics and culture.

Contents

PUBLISHER'S NOTE

We are very grateful for the unstinting help
received from Ralph Oppenhejm and
Ruth Lewis (son and daughter of the author)
and from Dina and Edward Ullendorff

Foreword

After her release from Theresienstadt and return to Denmark in 1945, Mrs Mélanie Oppenhejm lived another thirty-seven years until her death in 1982. Her account of life in that concentration camp focuses on the daily experiences of the hapless victims of Nazi cruelty, but she says little about her own sufferings and is much more concerned with those of her fellow-prisoners. Her story, though not intended as a scholarly or historical record, closely reflects what is now known about that infamous place.

Theresienstadt, situated at the point where the Eger meets the Elbe, was established as a Czech garrison town towards the end of the eighteenth century. Among the Czech soldiers there had always been a few Jews with their families. Between 1941 and 1945 it became a predominantly Jewish ghetto which was used, according to Nazi documents, to house the remnants of the Jewish population of Bohemia together with well-known and prominently well-to-do Jews from countries of Western Europe, in particular the Netherlands, Denmark and, of course, Germany and Austria. From Theresienstadt the inmates of the camp were gradually transferred to extermination camps, especially Auschwitz – as is harrowingly described by Mrs Oppenhejm.

The Germans tried to show off Theresienstadt as a 'model establishment', thus hoping to distract attention from the places where European Jews were inexorably being exterminated. To this end, in 1944 the Nazis took considerable trouble (as is shown in the central chapters of this book) to falsify the conditions of the inmates by setting up spurious schools, sham shops, cafés, gardens and temporary embellishments of all kinds – including even a bank with dud money, so-called 'Moses Scheine'. This was meant to deceive a Red Cross team of two Danish inspectors – not unknown to the Oppenhejms – into believing that this was a typical example of the new life of Jews under the Nazi regime. The international inspection was even followed by an SS film showing the spruced-up camp during the brief period of its fraudulent embellishment. Thereafter conditions reverted to their customary state of horror, starvation and squalor.

According to Dov Kulka's article in the *Encyclopaedia Judaica*, the population of the Theresienstadt concentration camp fluctuated greatly from month to month, but at its height some 53,000 people were crowded into 115,000 square metres, i.e. one inmate to every 2.16 square metres of space. Some 33,000 persons died in Theresienstadt itself and about 88,000 were transferred to extermination centres. When the camp was liberated in 1945, 11,000 persons were found alive; 413 of the 456 deported Danish Jews had survived and had already been rescued by the Swedish and Danish Red Cross. It seems that the Danes had fared better than most.

The internal administration of the camp was largely left in the charge of the Jewish Council of Elders, presided over by the Judenältester who was appointed by the German commandant. The most prominent among these chief executives was Paul Eppstein (1901–44), who had been Rabbi Leo Baeck's right-hand man on the Jewish Representative Council in Berlin. The most diabolical duty assigned to the chief Jewish elder was the selection of those to be sent on to the extermination camps. In September 1944, Eppstein (who had allegedly been nominated Judenältester on Eichmann's orders) was tortured and shot, as it was believed that he had been organising a self-defence unit among the inmates. His exposed position in the Theresienstadt establishment had caused him the gravest and most profound conflicts of conscience – as is movingly described by Mrs Oppenhejm in her book.

Rabbi Leo Baeck (1873–1956), after a life of distinguished religious service and scholarship, was called from a position of self-effacement to the apex of leadership of the Jews in Germany during the Hitler period. Even the Gestapo somehow sensed his saintly personality and carefully abstained from violating his dignity. He resisted all blandishments and calls to senior appointments abroad and vowed to remain with the last *minyan* (prayer quorum of ten) of Jews in Berlin. When finally he was taken to Theresienstadt as late as 1943, he was at once named honorary president of the Council of Elders. Baeck's biographer, Leonard Baker (*Days of Sorrow and Pain*, OUP, New York 1978), describes his subject's situation at Theresienstadt in terms which closely complement Mrs Oppenhejm's description in this book, although she does not actually refer to Baeck by name. Her story, taken in conjunction with the travail and fate of men such as Baeck and his former chief executive Eppstein, cannot but be read with emotion.

EDWARD ULLENDORFF
Oxford
Spring 2000

Preface

As if by a miracle, my mother Mélanie Oppenhejm survived nearly two years' detention in the concentration camp of Theresienstadt – a gigantic experiment in all the unimaginable evil of which human beings are capable. She endured this in company with my father, Overretsagfører (senior member of the Danish judicial system) Morits Oppenhejm, who had for decades acted, *inter alia*, as legal adviser to the German Embassy in Denmark. Two of their four children, their younger daughter and myself, were with them. We were rescued in 1945 thanks to the massive efforts of the Danish government, the Royal House and our fellow citizens.

After her return home my mother referred very rarely to what she had suffered in that man-made hell on earth. Once the family had returned to civilised life, she was reluctant either to dwell on memories of those macabre experiences or to burden her two elder children, who had escaped deportation and imprisonment, with allusions to those events.

Despite deteriorating health as a result of the many months of starvation and of forced labour for the Nazi armaments industry, she threw herself again with fervent energy into rescuing refugee children of the post-war era. That work was a resumption of her initiative, undertaken in the late 1930s, of bringing Jewish children from Germany, Czechoslovakia and Austria to Denmark. Her success in hundreds of cases she owed to the tireless support of Danish women's organisations.

All those *émigré* children survived the war, many as the sole members of their families to do so.

A year before my mother's death, the children who had remained in Denmark after the war invited her and their former foster-parents, mostly Danish farmers, to a party in Copenhagen. On that occasion the well-known journalist Thyra Christensen persuaded my mother to talk about the background of that reunion in a series of radio interviews. When these interviews were broadcast they aroused such great interest that this small volume came into being.

My mother used to tell me with some pride of her great-great-grandfather who, in 1806, had rescued the Prussian Queen Louise and her children (two of them became Kings of Prussia and one, Tsarina of Russia) on their flight from Napoleon's armies through Markish-Friedland. My mother had herself rescued hundreds of persecuted children, but far from being proud of this, she always lamented that she had not succeeded in saving many more before the occupation of Denmark by German troops in 1940 put a stop to what had hitherto appeared their only chance of rescue.

RALPH OPPENHEJM

CHAPTER I

The Nazi Menace

Parents from Germany, Poland and Czechoslovakia wrote to us: 'We beg you to give a home to our children, for we turn to you in fear for their lives and future.' That was in the 1930s. How was it conceivable, in that day and age, that parents were forced to get rid of their children in order to save them from a fate worse than separation?

In Germany, during the late 1930s, these children were no longer allowed to sit on benches in the park, or go to the beach for a dip, or visit the zoo. They were prevented from attending state schools. Their parents' books had been burnt in the early days of Nazi oppression. Now they were excluded from everything – because they were Jews. Parents became increasingly aware that the situation was hopeless. But no one could imagine that the Jews would be deported to concentration camps and exterminated by gas.

Some of the children who fled to Denmark at that time still live there now and meet frequently. In 1980 they invited us to a party. By now many of the seventy-seven who attended had children and grandchildren of their own. They sat in the hall of the Amager Library, some holding hands with their former foster-parents. They had become artisans, academics, farmers, dockers . . . others had gone into business or business-related occupations. I like to think they all contributed to Danish society.

I will tell you how all this came about. There was a lady in Germany who saw clearly what was going on. Her name was Recha Freier. After the Nazis seized power in 1933, she endeavoured to get Jewish children out of Germany; their ages ranged from fourteen to seventeen. Recha Freier had been born and bred in Germany, her ancestors having lived there for more than three hundred years. One day in the early 1930s she was going for a walk in the park with her parents. On the entrance gate was a notice: 'No admission for dogs or Jews'! She realised at once what would happen soon; but many Jews, who for generations had been living in Germany and contributing to its prosperity, failed to see how threatening Nazism was becoming to them and their families. And the rest of the world had no clear notion of what was going on in that country, either then or indeed later.

Recha Freier understood that she had to find a way to save Jewish children while there was still time. She turned to London where a committee had recently been formed to take care of Jewish refugees. This group of people, headed by Lord Balfour and other well-known British personalities, was endeavouring to place the children where there might be hope for their future. Their intention was to send Jewish children to the British mandated territory of Palestine where kibbutzim were labouring hard to reclaim and cultivate the desert.

The government of the Mandate did indeed grant permission for their entry into Palestine, provided that first and foremost they received thorough agricultural training – which should not, however, be paid for out of government resources. The cost of a two-year course per pupil amounted to some sixteen hundred Danish kroner (a great deal of money in those days); some set about collecting funds in all neutral European countries and in the United States of America. At the end of the two-year period the children would be expected to fend for themselves.

Since there were too many to be sent to Palestine all at once, Recha Freier thought that in the meantime they might be placed in private homes in Holland, Belgium, England, Sweden and Denmark, where they would be taught and trained, particularly in agriculture.

From 1937 on, Danish committees gathered donations for the youth organisation Youth Aliyah (*aliyah* being the Hebrew term for 'ascent', in the sense of 'ascending to the Holy Land'). Then on 9 November 1938 came the 'Kristallnacht', when hordes of Nazis went on the rampage in Germany, destroying synagogues, ransacking and pillaging Jewish shops and businesses and meting out unspeakable brutality. Earlier they had made bonfires of the books of Heine and other Jewish writers.

We realised that something had to be done at once. Fortunately, I had some very good friends, among them Kirsten Gloerfelt-Tarp, the head of the National Council of Danish Women. I turned to her in the days after the Kristallnacht; she was wonderful in her helpfulness and energy – as were Nina Andersen, a Member of Parliament and one of the leaders of the Social Democratic Party, and Else Zeuthen of the International League of Women for Peace and Freedom. Together with Thora Daugaard, the head of the International League for Peace and Freedom, we went to the Minister of Justice, K. K. Steincke, and enquired whether it would be possible to bring a thousand children from Germany to Denmark. He became very pensive.

There were many at that time who wanted to seek refuge in Denmark, but there was a good deal of domestic unemployment and people were afraid that the children would be employed on the land, thus depriving others of work. Since we were merely requesting entry permits for a two-year period to train these children in agriculture in order to send them subsequently to Palestine, Steincke became gradually more favourably inclined towards the project and agreed to bring twenty-five children to Denmark. The first of these arrived in June 1939. By the time of the German occupation of Denmark in April 1940, we had brought four hundred and fifty children into the country.

Soon after the Kristallnacht all fifty Women's Organisations, which were part of the National Council of Danish Women, set to work. Fundraising and meetings were organised, there were demonstrations against the Germans and homes were founded to accommodate the children. The International League of Women for Peace and Freedom was particularly active in searching for foster homes. Members travelled all over the country, explaining what was happening in Germany and why it was necessary to seek places of refuge for children. During our first journey, three hundred people in the countryside as well as in the towns offered them homes.

It was fairly complicated to bring these children across. Each one needed documents. In order to obtain these, we had to see K. K. Steincke time and again. Whenever we returned he seemed to want to say: 'This is the end now! I am going to throw you out, I want to see no more of you!' But we persevered.

There was one incident I shall never forget: we were in Gedser to take delivery of a group of children. The numbers had to correspond exactly to those listed and there was a little redhead, the brother of one of the children, who was not on the list. He had simply been put on the train. Well, of course, there were discussions and debates, a lot of toing and froing, before we managed to get him into Denmark. 'I shall have a word with Steincke,' I said, 'let the boy come along!' They let him through – the police of Gedser. But the extra boy had to be kept secret until everything had been properly arranged, so as to avoid problems later on when he was to go to Palestine.

Gradually people like Poul Reumert, Niels Bohr, Poul

Henningsen, university presidents, members of professional organisations, priests, doctors, students, journalists and many others started publishing articles about the situation in Germany and about the refugee children. The news that help was needed spread like wildfire throughout the country. When the German occupation came in 1940 – taking us all by surprise – it never occurred to anyone to leave the children in the lurch. On the contrary, this was an added reason to shield and to protect them.

I must say that the police, the day after the occupation, acted in an exemplary manner. On 10 April they despatched a police vehicle to me – a veritable Black Maria. I had in my possession a number of card indexes relating to the children, one of which I handed over to the police. A second one I burnt in the fireplace at home in Rungsted. It was generally assumed that the files would be safe in the custody of the police. I do not know whether the Germans ever found them when they took charge of the police records.

By great good fortune, during the occupation some officers in the Danish police enabled me to travel to Sweden on two occasions, each time with about forty children. All other routes abroad were now barred by the Germans. The idea was to send the children from Sweden via Russia and Syria to Palestine, but on arrival in Sweden we were unable to get permits for entry into Russia. However, I managed to arrange a meeting with the Russian envoy, Alexandra Kollontaj, a sympathetic and highly intelligent woman, who on both occasions used her influence on our behalf, and each time within two days we had the desired permits and the children travelled via Finland to Russia; but how they proceeded from there we never knew.

Some got out of Denmark in quite different ways. We had hoped to send batches of children to Marseilles, and thence by boat to Palestine, but owing to the occupation of France this proved impossible. There was, however, a very determined

Dutch lady, Gertrud Weissmuller, who came over from Holland and declared: 'I shall make sure that once the children get to Amsterdam they will be able to escape to Marseilles.' To begin with, however, it seemed quite impossible to obtain the necessary documents from the French Embassy in Copenhagen. I said I would stay put and not move an inch, day or night, until I had obtained the visas. Eventually I succeeded and about forty-five children got away to Amsterdam and from there, we hoped, to Marseilles and Palestine.

A very tricky situation arose when, during the German occupation (I think in about 1942), I was called to the Foreign Ministry where the German representative Renthe-Fink and Foreign Minister Erik Scavenius demanded the immediate removal from West Jutland of at least some of the refugee children there. Apparently military activity was expected to spread further. We had to find new homes for the children without delay – but this presented no problem at all. New doors were opening despite the risks the foster-parents were running.

The youngsters were at times difficult to manage, which was understandable after all they had been through. You could hardly expect fourteen- to seventeen-year-old adolescents, suddenly bereft of their parents, to be on their best behaviour. They neither knew the language nor the Danish way of life. They had come from cities like Berlin, Vienna or Prague, and now they were expected to move yet again. But they and their foster-parents made every effort to adjust to each other, and in most cases they succeeded.

Sometimes it didn't work and then they wrote to us; others just turned up at our home in Rungsted. They came from all parts of the country, and one evening there were seven or eight of them gathered at our house, unwilling to return to the places where they had been staying. What was to be done? We carted mattresses to provide bedding for the night, and our own children doubled up to make room for these guests. I telephoned the various foster-parents and asked them to allow the children to stay with us until the following day. The youngsters told us of their experiences, explaining all that they had had to leave behind them in Germany. Some of the foster-parents expected the children to adapt at once to their new life in Denmark, but many of them had come from totally different cultural backgrounds and reacted with bewilderment. They begged us to find somewhere else for them to live and this meant that after all the trouble we had taken we now had to start afresh in the search for new homes.

I recall, for instance, one boy who caused us a lot of difficulty. He just could not fit into the household on the island of Fyn where he was staying. He was very independent and precocious. Those in charge of him had expected him to do as he was told. One day he ran away; he had no money but managed the crossing to Copenhagen by stowing away on a ferry. Late one evening he arrived on our doorstep. His name was Otto. He was eventually captured by the Germans, and later on we were to find ourselves together in Theresienstadt – a concentration camp in Czechoslovakia.

Thirty-eight of the children who had found refuge in Denmark were seized by the occupation forces – despite all our efforts to keep them in hiding. During the Nazi campaign to round up Danish Jews, at the beginning of October 1943, German patrol vehicles went up and down the country in their search for the refugee children; some of them were caught fleeing across the fields. We had despatched warnings to the foster-parents. Fanny Arnskov of the International League of Women for Peace and Freedom tried to get some of the children away from the rural areas and to find safe havens for them. Many were brought to Gilleleje where they were concealed in the church to await a chance of escape to Sweden.

Alas, they were betrayed and sent to the internment camp of Horserød.

My husband and I, along with our two younger children, Ellen aged seventeen and Ralph eighteen, were arrested by the Germans on 1 October 1943. Together with others we had been trying to flee by boat to Sweden, but we were seized by a Danish captain and transported to Horserød. On 13 October we were deported to Theresienstadt. My elder son had been fortunate enough to escape in his kayak across the Øresund. My elder daughter was in London at the outbreak of war and stayed there for the duration. The seventeen-year-old refugee boy Otto was with us in the cattle wagon which took us to the concentration camp in Czechoslovakia, his country of origin. Despite the universal hopelessness in that cattle truck Otto remained firm in his belief that in his homeland he would see his parents again.

CHAPTER 2

Transportation to Theresienstadt

Nowadays one hears a great deal of refugees and persecutions, but in the past one knew little about such things, for in civilised countries they were virtually unknown. In those days one thought of Germany as a civilised country, the land of poets and thinkers. And now here we (and many others with us) were being arrested by the Germans despite the strenuous efforts of the Danes to transfer to Sweden as many of their Jewish fellow-citizens as possible.

We were being transported to Theresienstadt together with Danish internees from Horserød. At Warnemünde we were loaded into German cattle trucks. The floorboards were strewn with muck. We could neither sit nor lie down. Some people fainted, others were in a state of shock. They could not comprehend what had befallen them; it was all so grotesquely unreal – to be simply carted away like a sack of potatoes. Away with them, away from their cosy homes and normal lives! What were they supposed to have done? They had been ordinary, law-abiding citizens, members of Danish society, many of them from families that had been living in that country for two hundred and fifty years. They knew they had done nothing wrong at all, had committed no crime – and yet they were being arrested. If they had been guilty of fraud or of any other misdeed, punishment would not have come as a surprise. But all these old people, what had they done to be so brutally carried off? And what of the younger ones? What misdemeanour were they accused of? – let alone the little children, who could not even grasp what was happening.

The first thing we saw, after enduring a long day and a half in the cattle trucks, was a small station called Bauschowitz. Here we were let out to march on to Theresienstadt, a garrison town on the Eger, amidst the Bohemian mountains. It was a veritable fortress, built in 1780 by Emperor Joseph II of Austria and named after his mother, the Empress Maria Theresa. The complex had been constructed to accommodate about seven thousand soldiers. We saw a row of once smart but now rather dilapidated barracks, a few small houses for merchants, and some brothels. That was about all.

The first inmates we encountered were transport workers. On their shabby clothing they wore a yellow star with the word *Jude* (Jew) on it. They looked thin and ashen.

On arrival at the camp we were first made to pass through a sort of channel. We stood there, totally exhausted after the long journey during which we had not been permitted to leave the train even for an instant or allowed the means to clean up a bit. And now the Germans demanded answers in writing to all manner of questions. 'How many silver spoons and forks do you have at home? How many quilts, sheets, carpets, clocks, etc., etc.? Do you have money in the bank? What is the number of your account?' This went on for hours. How could one in those circumstances possibly recall what household utensils one had owned?

Thereafter they took all our belongings from us. The Danish police officers at Horserød had generously supplied us with food parcels, but even these were taken away. The only item which I was lucky enough to conceal was a tin of sardines, which the four of us shared for two or three days, after which the tin served as a water container.

Forty thousand people were, unbelievably, crammed into

that camp. There was a great crush of people walking, and people lying down. We saw nothing but emaciated faces; we heard nothing but noise. And the stench was unbearable! Just think, we had come from normal and hygienic circumstances. And now we encountered people who appeared to be moving at an unimaginably slow pace, as if in slow motion. We were at a loss to understand: why did all those thousands of people walk in such a peculiar way? What was the matter with them? Well, they were hungry. They just could not walk any faster. I well remember, about two weeks later, standing at the top of some stairs and looking down. I thought: how do I get down there? Of course, I did get down. I had to, because we were forced to go to work. But we had become so enfeebled.

During the first few days we just could not stomach the food they gave us. There was a sort of soup stagnating in an oil vat. People would queue for hours to obtain some of that tepid brew. It consisted of boiled potato peelings and heaven knows what else – scraps of turnip or whatever. But one thing is certain: we got used to it. And before long we were as keen as the rest of them to stand in line for hours to get our ration of that liquid. But it was revolting, and at first we just could not get it down. The prisoners who had been there for some time and become accustomed to the conditions took us to task: what did we expect? So we came to terms with things.

One day we were standing in the freezing cold waiting for the soup. An elderly gentleman was dishing it out – a precise measure apportioned to each one. A hat had fallen into the soup, but nobody was bothered about a bit more filth; we calmly ate the soup in which the hat was floating. I remember I was one of the last and received the dregs at the bottom of the vat. In the end, the man fished out the hat and wrung it out. Can anyone in the world, coming from a civilised life, imagine such squalor? But these things were happening and we came to accept them.

Hunger drives people to despair. No one who has not literally been starving can even begin to understand what it means to be really hungry. When you read about the poor starving poet in his garret writing melancholy poems by candlelight, you think to yourself: My God, dear poet, you have nothing to complain about! You could, after all, go to a shop and maybe steal a loaf of bread; or beg one of your neighbours for a crust, a bowl of soup, something to eat.

In Theresienstadt you could do no such thing. There was nothing to be had beyond the pitifully meagre ration.

CHAPTER 3

Meeting Fellow Inmates

On our first evening we were taken to the cellar of a dilapidated house. There were some ten or twelve bunks on one of which was seated a forlorn-looking man whom we knew. He was Judge Julius Moritz from Assens. When he saw us he gasped, 'Oppenhejm, you here? Carted away like us by the Germans? Just consider: a royal Danish judge and a senior member of the Danish bar! How *could* this happen? How *could* this come about? My sister is also here. She contracted pneumonia, so they put her in what passes for a sickbay. And I am just sitting here . . . '

Goodness me, poor Judge Moritz would have to get used to many things which, with his lack of imagination, he could never have envisaged – including the fact that he and his sister would have to share their accommodation with us and several others! One has to remember that this was many years before the idea of communal living was ever heard of. So he said to my husband, 'I could not possibly lie next to your wife. That would be quite improper; I cannot do that!' But he could and did and, little by little, things worked out.

Later his sister joined us. She was still ill but was getting better. She was a most peculiar person: every evening, when the rest of us arrived at our block exhausted from work, brother and sister would settle down and sing patriotic songs. That was the last thing we wanted to do to keep our spirits up. On the contrary, we felt emotionally too vulnerable to think of the past – recalling what once had been was quite unendurable. Most of the Danes felt that way. Others simply shut their eyes to reality and buried themselves in their memories. Judge Moritz and his sister never came to terms with the situation. Every day when they went for their food, he would say to his sister, 'Come, let us go to Tivoli.'

There was a small stove in our block. In the evening when my daughter and I returned from work outside the camp, we would pass by the SS barracks. There, out in the open, were mountains of coal. It was usually late, after dark, when we got there. One evening we fell upon that heap and picked up a few lumps which we concealed in our underwear. When we got back, we were at last able to light a fire.

Presently, Judge Moritz asked me, 'Where did you obtain that coal? Where did you buy it?'

'Buy it?' I said, 'what could I have bought it with? No, I pinched it fairly and squarely.'

He flushed and declared with indignation, 'Mrs Oppenhejm, you cannot expect a royal Danish judge to stay in a room heated with stolen coal.'

'You know, Judge Moritz,' I retorted, 'if you cannot manage that, you will just have to go outside; we are not going to freeze to death in temperatures of minus twenty.'

He became somewhat thoughtful. One evening when we returned to our barracks, he greeted us with a beaming smile. 'I have just purchased some firewood,' he said.

'Purchased?' I asked. 'How did you do that? You would not by any chance have paid for it with your bread?'

'What makes you think that?'

'What else could you have done? After all, you possess nothing with which to buy anything.'

'Two young men approached me and offered me some firewood in exchange for a piece of bread,' he admitted.

I then had a very serious word with him: 'Judge Moritz, you

are a thousand times worse than me. My daughter and I are honest thieves. But do you know what you are? You are a receiver of stolen goods. The young people had, of course, stolen the firewood. And you paid for it with bread which you really could not spare!'

He was completely speechless and very shaken. He was still having difficulty adapting to the conditions he was confronted with in a world far removed from his former orderly juristic life in Denmark, where normal rules and standards had prevailed, where right was right and wrong was wrong. He was now a picture of such utter misery that my husband went to comfort him, making it clear that warmth was worth infinitely more than moral principles; they might apply elsewhere but not here.

There were a thousand things, petty in themselves, which would assume the utmost importance – inconceivable to anyone living in normal circumstances.

One evening the lights were left on. Usually they were turned off quite early. On this occasion a transport of inmates was to be dispatched, and so our block remained lit up. We watched Miss Moritz undress, her hair loosened. My son said to her, 'Truly, Miss Moritz, you bear a remarkable resemblance to Queen Caroline Mathilde, the mother of Frederick VI [of Denmark].'

Brother and sister blushed a deep red, though we could not guess why. Greatly embarrassed they later confided to us that one of their great-great-grandmothers had been the illegitimate child of King Frederick VI. We bombarded them with questions and wanted to know why they had not told the Germans about that on arrival. They might have been released and returned home. After all, it was known how deferential the Germans were towards anyone connected with royal blood. But they said they had lacked the courage to do so and kept quiet because they were too ashamed. We felt that surely no blame attached to them on account of their poor great-great-grandmother.

So the following day my husband went to see the camp commandant. It was just possible that these were sufficient grounds to effect their release. But it was no use – it was too late now. They should have made a declaration about that at the time of their arrest, with evidence confirming their descent and proving conformity with the specific criteria laid down by the Nazis. Now they were here and were here to stay.

Such matters were apt to come to light in almost comical ways in the face of all the vileness around us and the truly horrendous circumstances in which we found ourselves. It surpassed everything one had ever read or heard about such a place and such conditions. Yet there were still things that made us laugh, so tragicomic and farcical did they appear against the background of our present situation.

I keep referring to 'Judge' Moritz; although we lived in such close proximity for nearly two years, we continued with the formal mode of address and the use of titles. This was typical of our behaviour and conduct in the camp in general. It was as if in that hell on earth we all had the need to cling to customs and traditions reminiscent of our former civilised existence. In the past, in our ordinary lives, we had not taken matters of etiquette quite so seriously.

CHAPTER 4

Learning to Cope

The refugee boy Otto didn't find his parents in the concentration camp. They had been deported from there long before our arrival. Of all his family only one uncle remained and he was a great solace to the boy. A few of the children who had been with us in Denmark did meet some of their relations in Theresienstadt, but in most cases the families had disappeared. Every now and again some of the children came across an inmate who was able to tell them of their relatives' fate.

The Czech children who had earlier found refuge with us in Denmark now became our link with the outside world – a world from which we had been cast out. Many of those children were used by the Germans to work on the land. They were guarded by Czech gendarmes who would talk to them in their own language whenever they were out of earshot of the SS. These gendarmes were not all bad, for they, too, lived in fear, not knowing what their eventual fate would be. So we obtained a little bit of news about what was happening; thus we heard of the Normandy landings and what had happened to Mussolini. However, precise news was hard to come by because many of these gendarmes could neither read nor write.

Otto was considered unique in Theresienstadt. Often in the evenings he would visit us and dig deep in his trouser pockets to pull out a few potatoes, all of which had bite marks. He had pinched them from the pigsty in the yard beyond the camp where he was slaving for the SS. By God, we ate them! We ate them greedily. It was an unforgettable gesture, for the boy could have kept them for himself; he showed rare selflessness in circumstances where each individual, for the most part, looked after his own interests.

It was minus twenty degrees, and we had no fuel to heat our barracks. Otto came to the rescue, bearing a large tree trunk which he had stolen from the Germans. Since he could not conceal this under his jacket, he was in great danger of discovery while delivering it to us. But how were we to chop up that tree? We had no tools. Then someone produced a pocket knife. How do you cut up a tree trunk with a pocket knife? Needless to say, the knife broke in two and we were left with half a pocket knife with which to shave wood off the tree. Once again, Otto solved the problem; he produced some sort of implement he had nicked from the Germans with which we could cut up the trunk. At last we had firewood for our little stove, also stolen, for which my husband had made a flue, the pipe of which was sticking out of a window.

The bread issued to us was revolting, full of waste material and completely inedible. But it helped if we toasted the slices and hung them up beside the stove. Of course, invariably they dropped down on to the dirty floor. Nevertheless, we thought they made a delicious meal. And when people fell ill with dysentery, which frequently happened, then the burnt bread acted as a kind of charcoal pill.

CHAPTER 5

The Inferno

It was many months before we received parcels from Denmark; until then we had to make do with what we were given in the camp. The weekly ration for each was half a loaf of bread, consisting of waste material, potato peelings and some sort of 'flour' made of a mixture of bark or rind which the Germans would not use for themselves. The bread was issued to the 'house-elder', who was in charge of order and discipline in the block; he also had to enforce compliance with all the rules and regulations.

We had, for instance, those multi-bunk beds, and we were forbidden to put anything on the floor. The pitiful blankets we had been given (we did, in fact, use our coats and any other possessions as bedcovers) had to be folded in neat parcels according to strict guidelines, always ready for a possible SS inspection. Nothing was allowed to protrude; on our bunks we kept shoes and bread – if we had any – and our weekly ration of margarine, which was smaller than a finger. And all that would get gummed up with the dirty rags. We received a very little sugar, a few grams per week, which we stored on little tin plates, or whatever miserable utensils we had, and kept under our bedclothes; no one was allowed to see what we possessed. It was such a mishmash and an unbelievable mess. However, we tried to keep things tidy, as best we could.

But how were we to rid ourselves of the fleas? The straw

mattresses and the cracks in the floorboards were teeming with fleas. We would all sit together and, without any embarrassment, we would search under our skirts and the men would rummage in their trousers in an effort to squash the fleas. We seldom succeeded.

But worst of all were the bedbugs. On our first night in the cellar my daughter started scratching. And soon everyone was scratching. It sounded like a concert from another planet, and it went on night after night. Bugs don't only bite, they also have a nasty smell. We had nothing, absolutely nothing, to use as a spray, and every evening, with the onset of darkness, the bugs appeared and with them the fleas. Apart from being a constant torment, they were also a health hazard in that they carried infectious diseases and caused inflammations. We were always tired and exhausted but could never properly sleep at night; then early next morning we had to get up and start work again.

Water had to be carried from a long distance away. And then there were the latrines, those disgusting, filthy latrines; they were lined up in rows of twelve and many times we would be ordered to clean them. We received commands for all sorts of dreadful tasks. Registering deaths was one of my husband's duties as part of 'running the environment'; this also included managing the living quarters and billets. The Germans demanded masses of statistics, but for whose benefit? The dead were made to vanish from sight, and their bunks were immediately allocated to other prisoners or new arrivals. Everything had to be recorded and accounted for, not least to prevent anyone getting hold of any scrap of the meagre rations to which he or she was not entitled.

One evening a transport from Holland arrived, among them some people we happened to know. Most of them were to be sent on. There was a mother with two daughters: the daughters were selected for the onward transportation. The mother turned to us and begged us to hide her children. But how were we to do that? Someone once tried to hide in the latrines, but he was discovered and immediately sent to the 'little fortress' outside Theresienstadt. That was where people were taken to be tortured or killed.

My son was commanded to assist at operations for a month. He had never in his life been present at a surgical operation. The following month he was ordered to carry away dead bodies. That was the job that needed to be done most frequently in Theresienstadt. There were some old hearses from the days of the Austrian Empire and very handsome they were too. They were pulled by the prisoners. As a rule, they were used for the distribution of bread to the various blocks. The loaves were piled in stacks, and a certain number was delivered to each block and handed over to the elders. After that, the same carriages were used to collect the corpses, and the corpses lay there as still as the loaves, mustered in much the same way. The bodies were taken to the crematorium to be burnt and the ashes were put in cardboard boxes with names written on them. The boxes were then taken elsewhere to be stored in stacks.

While my son was working as porter of bread and bodies, my daughter was assigned to all manner of tasks. Every evening each of us was given a note which stated where we had to attend next morning. She was ordered to work as a cleaner and to supervise some disturbed children who were running about. There were swarms of children whose parents had been deported, while others had reached Theresienstadt quite alone. These were little children, many of whom were later sent to the extermination camp at Auschwitz. There were some among us who would look after the children and see to it that they had something to do; there were no books, and there was nothing to write with. There was absolutely nothing. Teaching was strictly forbidden; but we organised it clandestinely.

On another occasion my daughter was put to work on mica. I was there, too. Mica is a mineral found in the mountains of Czechoslovakia. At the time we had no idea what its use was. It was apparently processed for the war industry – something to do with aircraft. I do not know in what capacity it was employed, whether it was needed for engines or what, but it was of great importance. Many of the female captives had to serve there, working day and night on that material. We were handed segments resembling whale-bladders which we had to split. How on earth does one split a whale-bladder? It is damned difficult. But we were ordered to do it, and there was to be no wastage whatsoever. Every piece of mica was weighed before we received it, and again when we returned it. It was to be split across, and if there was the least wastage – which was quite unavoidable – we were punished and had to do overtime. Again and again we would squat for ten or twelve hours on hard wooden benches, in freezing draughts and squalid conditions, crushing the mineral fragments. To begin with, the dust made our eyes smart and also affected our lungs and made breathing difficult. Our hands hurt, and our fingers went numb. And all the while we had to sing in case some of the 'Herren' SS officers passed by to check what a wonderful time we were having, singing songs and toiling away at the mica and pretending to be blissfully happy. In Theresienstadt squalor and misery had to be depicted as idyllic. It was all a campaign of lies. The whole camp was a scenario such as Dante must have envisaged when writing his *Inferno*.

CHAPTER 6

The Aged

What sort of people were we – we who were forced to languish in a concentration camp? Were we the sub-humans we were portrayed as by Hitler? Certainly not, such a thought never occurred to us. Were we to be robbed of our dignity by hunger, vermin, humiliation and fear? Were we to be driven to mean and indecent behaviour and become the type of creatures which the Nazis had branded us?!

Among the inmates there were, of course, small-minded and selfish people who never missed an opportunity to browbeat others and to steal their food or their boots or whatever they could lay their hands on. But there were also many, very many, who not only kept their dignity and humanity, but were also admirable in their efforts to make a barbaric life just a little more humane.

I am thinking particularly of the old people, men and women who had been deported from Denmark, among them Rosa Kielberg, Rose Hartvig, Irma Hertz, Louis Bramson, Sara Merklin, Bolette Levy, Rigmor Adler and so many others. All the older people from Denmark were banished to the attic, that vast loft under the roof of the barracks. And there they lay! There were hardly any blankets and no medicines. These people behaved magnificently and tried to help each other. Those in the windowless corners were always lying in the dark. Only those sleeping near the tiny windows in the roof got a bit of light. In winter it was freezing cold, while in summer the heat was unbearable.

It was, however, quite remarkable how these human beings retained their dignity in spite of everything. When we went to see how they were keeping, they enquired instead how we were and how our children were faring, and whether we had any news from home. They rarely complained, not even when they lacked warmth or indeed water. Many of them were lying on sacks of straw on bare floorboards among total strangers.

How were they to fetch a bucket of water when they could not manage the many stairs? How were they to wash themselves in that cold? It was truly uplifting to see how these people, in those conditions, beset by fleas and other vermin, remained human and did not sink into self-pity.

CHAPTER 7

Paul Eppstein

There was a gentleman at Theresienstadt whom we had known previously, the economist Dr Paul Eppstein. He had been chief executive of the Representative Council of the Jews in Germany (Reichsvertretung der Deutschen Juden). He and his wife Hedwig had visited us in Denmark before the war and had helped us bring over Jewish children from Germany, Austria and Czechoslovakia.

In Theresienstadt, as head of the Jewish Council of Elders, he acted as intermediary between the SS and the inmates. It was he who was charged by the SS with the main responsibility for ensuring that everything ran smoothly. He and his wife were assigned quarters which, compared with our own, were quite bearable. They had, for example, such unusual things as chairs. He would ask us to spend the odd hour with them and we could enjoy the rare luxury of sitting on real chairs and stretching our legs. All the time Eppstein was deeply depressed. He was one of the few who knew what fate awaited the inmates once they were taken from Theresienstadt.

The news that 'transports' were being prepared invariably meant that Eppstein had been commanded to select three to four thousand people from among the inmates, as directed by the camp commandant: a specified number of men, women and children from each age group, so many disabled, war invalids, consumptives, orphans, etc. They all had to go. Often

37

husbands and wives would be separated – if, for example, one of the spouses was doing a specialist job or the SS wished to retain that person in Theresienstadt for one reason or another. Parents were not always permitted to leave together with their children – or vice versa – even when they volunteered to go. Not even in death were they allowed to be together. The notices arrived in the evening: prisoner number so and so was ordered off; number so and so likewise. And there would be great agitation and distress.

I frequently had to assist in these preparations. I was charged with removing prostheses. I had to unstrap artificial limbs and take out artificial eyes and teeth from living human beings. And then everything had to be sorted in precise order: artificial arms to the right, legs to the left. They were to be allocated to German soldiers. I had to deprive these wretched people of their precious aids. They had themselves served in the German army and had fought for the fatherland from 1914 to 1918. They had risked life and limb, and this was Germany's gratitude. Everything, absolutely everything, was taken away from them. How was a man without a leg or an arm to climb up on to those high cattle trucks? But it was done; people were pushed into those wagons by the loathsome Gestapo and SS men with their automatic weapons and dogs and whips. Those prisoners who were not quick enough would receive the lash of a whip or the kick of a boot.

Many times I remember standing there, unable to move, overcome with fury. Had I held a pistol in my hand I could have shot those brutes without feeling any remorse. There they were, prancing, scoffing and making stupid jokes about those hapless people who almost certainly sensed what was to befall them but could do nothing about it. And all the time the German soldiers, the Gestapo and the SS men were standing about making fools of them. And if they felt so inclined, they would even snatch away their bundles.

It was beyond comprehension. After all, were those Germans not fellow human beings, with children, wives and parents? How could normal individuals behave in such a manner? Did they have no sense at all that these victims were people like them? But they had been brainwashed over many years to believe that they were supermen, members of a master race who could commit the most barbaric acts against other creatures as a right and a duty. Their behaviour passed the power of human understanding.

The cattle trucks were locked and sealed – and we stood by, paralysed with horror, unable to do anything, even to weep. Often the wagons would be left for two or even three days before being moved on. The German war machine was working at high pressure; the German railways were groaning under the weight of troops and provisions being carried to and from the eastern front. So those poor people in their cattle trucks had to wait for days on end, without food, without space to sit or to lie down. At the time we had no certain means of knowing what would happen to them, but we felt sure it was going to be monstrous. If they did not die of starvation they would die in some other atrocious way.

Prisoners in concentration camps could only guess at what was going on in the outside world. We knew nothing at all; we had no newspapers and no radio and had to rely on rumours and hearsay which we had in abundance. Paul Eppstein, on the other hand, was privy to much that was happening; and knowing the fate of the captives in the cattle trucks put him at risk. Otherwise there were only a few people in the camp who had any inkling of the existence of gas chambers. A story would soon begin to circulate, told by a man who had managed to escape from Theresienstadt: he was subsequently captured and sent to Auschwitz where he picked up whispered stories of extermination by gas. Inexplicably he was returned to Theresienstadt.

We simply could not believe Paul Eppstein when he first spoke of it. But gradually more and more rumours emerged, convincing us of the gruesome truth. We did not dare, we lacked the nerve, to pass on to our closest friends in the camp what Eppstein had recounted to us. We often thought that we could never tell anyone about it. Sometimes we wondered whether such enormities were even possible. Today we know that they were. But at the time, not being certain that the unspeakable was actually being committed, we did not dare to think such thoughts – let alone share them with others who were already deeply depressed. But the suspicions remained. And then another four thousand were deported; and next time the number had risen to five thousand.

At Christmas transports to the extermination camps seemed to cease, and the few God-fearing Christians among the inmates firmly believed that at long last the Lord had seen what was happening to us and the cessation of transports was a sign that He was coming to our aid. Then Christmas passed. The German engine drivers and the SS men had, of course, simply been enjoying a short Christmas holiday. But hardly had the festive season ended than the transports resumed – journeys into the unknown, into suffering of a magnitude that is still unimaginable to us today.

Human beings are extraordinary creatures. They hope and hope and never give up hope. They were all convinced that soon there would be an end to the misery. Rumours that the Russians or the British were about to liberate us were rife, but the rumours were wrong.

Harassment was a daily occurrence. We had, for example, to wear the Star of David on our clothing. Heaven help those who forgot to obey that rule! We were forced to affix that yellow star, with the word *Jude* in black letters, to our clothes; if we failed to do so – perhaps we had no needle or thread or a safety pin, or had simply forgotten – what then? We would be punished with kicks, beatings or detention. There might even be withdrawal of food rations, causing yet more hunger. It just did not make sense. Why on earth did we have to wear that Star of David? Our torturers knew full well that we were Jews, being detained in a camp which they delighted in describing as a Jewish settlement with autonomous Jewish administration, a veritable model camp where all were allegedly flourishing.

CHAPTER 8

Armistice Day 1943

How well we were supposed to be doing became pretty clear to us on 11 November 1943, about a month after our deportation. The Germans had never forgotten their defeat in 1918, and now they were bent on revenge. Armistice Day was 11 November, the day of the ceasefire in 1918. On the evening of 10 November the command went out that we were to hold ourselves in readiness at four o'clock next morning on the main road of the camp. The whole camp, all forty thousand prisoners, from small children to ninety-year-olds, had to report. We were then marched to a large field outside the camp and there we were counted to make sure, heaven help us, that no one was missing. We had no idea why we were being counted again; they did, after all, count us every evening.

And so we were assembled. It took a long time. We were mustered in rows. We had had no food and no water and were not allowed to stir. It was quite unbelievable. Forty thousand people standing in strict formation, toddlers and the very aged on crutches and sticks, in the freezing cold and rain. The SS men with their dogs were reviewing those lined up, and God help anyone who had the misfortune to stumble a bit. People were trembling with fear. If anyone moved a fraction to the right or left the SS would come with their whips and beat the culprit to the ground. He was, however, not permitted to stay there but was forced to get up. In addition, the person at the head of the formation would get a slap on the face which had to be passed on down the line.

Despite all this viciousness, the behaviour of the captives to each other was beyond compare. Each helped another whenever possible. I remember there was an old man standing in front of us, and my son stretched out his knee so that the poor old man could rest on it from time to time. But this could not be kept up for long, for if the Germans happened to pass by and notice, all hell would be let loose.

Suddenly that vast multitude, forty thousand people, were struck numb. The Nazis had fighter-bombers fly very low over the column. We believed that our last hour had come and that we were going to be mown down. Then, all of a sudden, after we had been standing there motionless for nearly sixteen hours, the aircraft disappeared. And now came the command: Everybody back! There followed tremendous jostling and pushing and indescribable panic. Yet it was as if the people were rejoicing to get home again – even if home was the camp. We all felt the urge for a roof over our heads, to lie down and shake the whole ghastly experience off – which, of course, was quite impossible.

The Czech gendarmes guarding us alongside the SS were considerably more humane than the Germans. They told some of the Czech inmates that British espionage had discovered that the Nazis had indeed intended to murder all those assembled on the field and had let it be known via the BBC that Britain would take retaliatory action. I have no idea whether there was any truth in that.

The long day on the icy field cost innumerable lives because many of the people were subsequently enfeebled by bouts of flu, kidney infections and pneumonia. The torments and harassment went on and on in every conceivable way to the despair of us all. Only those who have actually lived through such agonies themselves can imagine the horrors.

CHAPTER 9

Daily Life

Every day something disquieting occurred in the camp, something causing anxiety. There was never any peace of mind or atmosphere of calm. But suddenly the strong sense of impending disaster increased, as though some dire event was looming dangerously close. Then it was rumoured that Eichmann was to visit and we knew that, if he did, something dreadful would indeed happen. At that time we had no idea that it was he who was running the extermination apparatus, that he was at the apex of the entire murder industry. We feared him – strutting in his jackboots and spurs and carrying a whip which many a back was to feel. Then came the dreaded legacy of his visit: deportations! Everybody started packing. No one knew if this was the moment; it was like a lottery.

The aged crammed in the loft, the consumptives, the sick and infirm, all whose turn for transportation had come packed their meagre belongings. They tried to keep a few of their things with them; others they left with their friends. On one occasion we received the gift of a woollen blanket.

Those who were spared deportation did all they could to help others whose time for departure was imminent. They would share their food, of which they had precious little. And all of them asked themselves the same gruesome questions: Where are these people being dispatched? What will happen to them? Why are they being sent to the East?

44

A single Dane was attached to one of the transports – a mentally ill man. Nobody knows why the Danes in particular were not delivered to the by now notorious extermination camps. The Dutch, the Belgians and the French were not spared.

I suspect that fewer inmates would have died of sheer desperation and despondency had they known that in two or three years' time they would be liberated. They might have found the strength to survive had they been sure that they would see their children or their spouse or their parents again. How could we know what had happened to our children? For a long time we had no idea at all. And what had been the fate of all the men and women who happened to be away from their families when the Germans went on a manhunt all over Denmark? Had they all disappeared? Had they found refuge in Sweden? Had they been captured and were languishing in other concentration camps?

At long last we, the Danes, received a few postcards from Sweden and Denmark. In 1944 we learned that our elder son had succeeded in escaping to Sweden, and through him we received greetings from our daughter in London. We were strictly forbidden to write more than twenty-five words per month, and our postcards were inevitably censored. Shortly before the Danes had arrived in Theresienstadt, the Germans, so we were told, had hanged three Czechs in the marketplace for smuggling some letters from the starving in the camp to relatives in Prague. This was intended as a deterrent, a warning to others.

We would therefore write: 'Greetings to Mathilde Christensen!' (which was at the time a well-known delicatessen in Copenhagen) or 'All the best to Rubow!' (a popular bakery). Or we would say that we had been re-reading the book by Knut Hamsun, the work which had made his literary name. This was how we spelled out the idea of *hunger*. We were full of confidence and hope whenever we received a sign of life from outside. On one occasion a card decorated with bright blue forget-me-nots arrived which convinced us that Denmark was about to come to our aid; they had not forgotten us. Later it emerged that the person who had sent that card never dreamt that we would interpret it to mean: 'Now the worst is over and spring is at hand.' He had just fancied that pretty card picturing flowers he would like to have given us. We, however, were firm in our belief that salvation was coming, that help was on the way. But nothing happened, nothing at all. Things went on as before. There were more and more deportations and yet more arrivals.

Many Danes received postcards from Sweden and it became clear that their families had no clue of what was actually happening to us. The cards would tell of parties people had been to, of invitations to birthday celebrations or that little Johnny had had a cold and a runny nose. They hoped that the family in Theresienstadt were all right and thought that they should write a bit more often. These ordinary messages made many people terribly depressed – but there was so much else to worry about, first and foremost food.

After several months we received our first parcels from Denmark, sent by good friends. But what did the parcels contain? Clothing! Of course, we were freezing like dogs, but compared with hunger that was of secondary importance. We were bitterly disappointed.

Through its envoy in Berlin, Denmark had asked for permission to send food parcels to Danish citizens in Theresienstadt. At first the Germans, or the Gestapo, replied that the Danes were receiving the same rations as all the others in the camp, which, they alleged, were ample. Friends of ours, Dr Per Thygesen and his wife, had grave doubts about the adequacy of the food rations, so they obtained an export permit and went to the post office to dispatch the first parcels containing provisions. Fortunately, they were not the only private individuals who had enough nous and compassion to try and help us. Fully four months later, in February 1944, the first parcels arrived via the Red Cross. To take delivery of the gifts they contained we were forced to queue for hours. Everything was laboriously examined and there were searches for cigarettes and tobacco and medicines. Often the parcels were only half full because they had been plundered. Who were the thieves? Well, maybe somebody was so hungry that he could not resist helping himself. It goes without saying that the Germans had taken first choice.

Nevertheless, there usually was something left, just sufficient for survival. With some food in reserve, life for us was totally transformed. A few people were famished to such an extent that they devoured the whole lot in one go, as soon as they got it. Others, indeed most of us, used our delicacies sparingly, saving some with an eye to the future. Each time we asked ourselves whether there would be another parcel?

The inmates were not allowed to accept cigarettes or tobacco. Smoking was strictly forbidden; if anyone was discovered – and somebody would from time to time be caught with a dog-end – the penalty was rigorous imprisonment. One day a well-known man from Prague received a cigarette stub from a Czech gendarme, and that cost him six months' hard labour. The SS men themselves were running a black market and would now and again smuggle cigarettes into the camp. Whenever cigarette prices went down, the SS would organise a raid and punish those who were caught. Invariably this would push up the black-market prices.

And, oh dear me, the cheese in the food parcels frequently appeared to be alive! Sometimes it had been in transit for weeks or even months and it was full of mites, but that did not inhibit anyone from eating it. Somebody sent us eggs on one occasion. When eventually they reached us, they were a ghastly rotten mess. We howled with frustration and fury.

There was a rule which prevented us from receiving more than one parcel per month, and frequently it would be only half a parcel. Even the fat in a sausage could be of immeasurable value, if one cherished any hopes of survival. When the others saw that we had received a parcel, they would come along to congratulate us on our good fortune. Well, we had to share; we could not deny them, could we?

Occasionally, the packets would contain vitamin pills and medicines, but these had to be handed over. They would be sent back to Denmark as evidence that we had no need of such things. The Germans were taking care of us: indeed they took such care that the many who never received any extra food to supplement the camp rations would 'snuff it' – if I may be permitted to use such an expression.

We kept asking ourselves: why on earth had they bothered to drag people here – only to watch them die a slow death? Who can grasp or fathom that? Could they not have shot them straight away? But no, those who did not perish there and then – and there were thousands of them – would be packed into cattle trucks and finished off wherever it was that they were being taken to.

CHAPTER 10

Cultural Activities

Human beings are unpredictable creatures, and many are able to adapt to the most unbelievable situations. In the midst of this macabre absurdity and abiding disconsolateness people could still laugh and chat or attend lectures in the big attics of the barracks. Among the inmates who lectured there were famous professors and scholars. They talked about German poetry or the latest discoveries in chemistry; about French art or Roman law. And the audience enjoyed taking part in activities reminiscent of the outside world. In that way they could escape their misery for an hour or so. Other speakers might include actors, lawyers, painters and musicians – talking on anything that came to mind. The lecturers delivered their material with great attention to detail and at inordinate length. And the people squatted on the floor in the darkness and listened patiently. It was as if they derived strength from hearing about matters extraneous to their troubles.

There was a former Austrian colonel whom we had met when queuing endlessly for our soup. He was a born soldier, but he also wrote poetry. And in the evening he would turn up and ask whether he might have the honour to recite his poems. There were verses about flowers and about beautiful women; verses about the camp and about the dead.

He would begin thus: ' "Roses", a poem written by Colonel (retired) Alois Schrantzhofer, read on such and such a day for

49

Mr and Mrs Oppenhejm, Judge Moritz and his sister, and the wife of Commander Schultz.' And then he would recite his poetical creations, one after the other. Each would be prefaced by the name of a flower and then 'a poem written by Colonel (retired) Alois Schrantzhofer, read on such and such a day . . . ' Good Lord, the only consolation we could offer him was to listen patiently and to applaud in appreciation of his poems. On the whole, poetry did not exactly suit our frame of mind. Colonel Schrantzhofer was killed by a bomb that hit Theresienstadt shortly after we had left the camp in 1945.

There were several generals in the camp, mainly Austrian. One of them was the well-known Field Marshal Johann Franz Friedländer; he ended up in an extermination camp. There were all sorts of people at Theresienstadt; the Danes included several eminent personalities, such as old Mrs Schultz, Commander Schultz's wife. She was eighty-three years old and had her two daughters with her. She never gave any hint of how she felt and took everything in her stride. At the beginning of 1944 her daughters were sent home to Denmark because their father was Christian and so were they. That was evidently the only thing the Nazis took into consideration. This was both a great good fortune and a tragedy. The old lady had to be left behind on her own, and none of them dared hope they would ever meet again.

The daughters were desperately unhappy when they had to take leave of their mother. I clearly remember the day of their departure. Mrs Schultz had packed the little bit of bread in her possession for her daughters to take with them. After all, she could not know how long it would take them to reach Denmark. It was quite conceivable that the poor girls (they were then about my age, early forties) would receive no food or drink at all while travelling home under German control. She was worried sick about them.

The Germans would frequently organise interrogations and

subject people to questionings. Mrs Schultz had originally come from the West Indies but she was of Danish parentage. She insisted on speaking English only and would not yield – whether the Germans understood her or not. They just had to put up with it.

When the official Danish Red Cross Commission – to which I shall refer later – was expected to come to Theresienstadt, the Germans proposed moving Mrs Schultz into better quarters. They were apprehensive that the Danes might enquire about her because of her connection with the Royal House. Mrs Schultz was very outspoken, and the Germans were determined to prevent any risk of the members of the commission meeting her. They were concerned that the formidable old lady might tell the truth; hence she had to be got out of the camp. When the Nazis came to take her away, she said that if she had to leave she would go only to Denmark. But like all the rest of us she was compelled to obey the Germans.

When people wanted to enter or leave the building, they invariably had to pass our room. One of them, the head of the Danish Soldiers' Confederation, Carl Heine, would turn up every morning with some puns or wisecracks hoping to cheer us up. Mrs Schultz, who had been used to a different milieu, was not amused by his antics. Yet he could be quite funny. At night, the poor man lay on his bed wearing his round hat and his coat and red scarf because he had nothing at all to use as a bedcover. Nevertheless, he always said something to encourage us. Carl Heine had lost his teeth when the Germans had come to take him away, and there was no way he could obtain dentures. But who needed teeth when all we got was soup? He came to terms with the situation; and so did many others. Despite all the privations, misery, ill health and hopelessness, many people retained their sense of humour in such a measure that they could help others to bear the unbearable.

CHAPTER 11

Seeking Warmth

It was bitterly cold and we were freezing. What we managed to steal was insufficient to stoke our little stolen stove. From time to time we would go down to the cellar to visit Mr Reich who was living there with his charming wife and his daughter. Reich had come from somewhere near Prague, where he had been employed as a gardener. In Theresienstadt he was working for the Germans as an agricultural labourer, just outside the precinct. Every now and again he succeeded in bringing back a little firewood or coal, of which the Germans had enormous quantities. He would then be able to heat their tiny stove in the cellar and we would be invited down to join them sitting close together near the oven.

One of the party used to be an old man of seventy, also from Prague, who had been a teacher. To keep himself awake he would tell us stories about Rabbi Loew who, in the sixteenth century, had created an artificial being, the so-called Golem. And we would all tell stories, just to take our minds off reality.

Whenever we visited the Reichs they gave us a present. They had been able to rescue a few things from their home when they were taken away. On one occasion they gave us a blanket, which was a great comfort against the cold; on another we got a pillow. How could we thank these people? The only opportunity occurred when we received a parcel which we could share with them. They were so grateful.

One day Mr Reich came and told us that the Germans were

going to send him to work elsewhere. The family were naturally in despair: his wife was wretched with grief, as was his daughter. Like so many young women she was getting bloated as a consequence of undernourishment. Later he came up to bid us farewell. I was not on duty for this particular deportation and therefore I could not be present to say goodbye when they pushed him into the cattle truck. The Reichs were exceptionally refined people who never ever complained. Now he was gone, and the two women were left alone in the cellar.

CHAPTER 12

Prayers

There were many Orthodox Jews in the camp. Every painfully long day they held clandestine prayer meetings, firm in the belief that the day would come when the Lord would put an end to their suffering. But there were quite a number who did not pray. Having seen what was happening, they had lost their faith in divine providence. Many helped and encouraged each other to overcome their pessimism. Others fell victim to deepest despair and extreme anguish. No wonder when conditions were so utterly appalling. Imagine the filthy bunks where the bread was kept – amidst fleas and bugs – yet we actually ate it, we really did! Somebody told us that fleas tended to leap into water. We had a small tin which we filled with water and placed beside the bunks. And the fleas did indeed jump, but damn it all, not into the water but on to us! I can feel the stings to this day, as well as the nausea and the stench of the bedbugs at night.

Not only did all the vermin around us make us ill, they also made us very bad-tempered. We were often at the end of our tether and literally drained of lifeblood – the bugs would suck out what was left. The air was filled with stench and filth and noise. People were driven mad and reacted irritably if you so much as brushed against them inadvertently in the street where thousands were milling around. In their hopelessness and hunger, with their nerves jangling, people were scarcely aware what they were saying or doing. I keep recalling the

54

hunger and the fear which dominated everything, day and night.

When in the past we visited the Reich family in the cellar, we would meet another pleasant family (they came from Brünn) who shared their room. Their name was Lustig and they had twin sons aged sixteen or seventeen. Suddenly out of the blue one of those accursed orders arrived: the boys were to be sent to a labour camp. The name of the camp was Birkenau. Now, my husband and I had learnt from Paul Eppstein that Birkenau was close to Auschwitz, and we knew what was happening there. Mr Lustig was a clever and pleasant man, and his wife was charming and ever helpful. Stoically, they both accepted this blow and thought that, after all, the boys were young and had to work wherever the Germans decreed. Surely, the war could not last much longer and then they would all be reunited. We never saw the twins again. Shortly afterwards the parents, too, were removed. That was the end of the Lustig family.

There was one young couple I shall never forget. On the point of deportation they asked a rabbi whether he could marry them according to the Law – not the German law but the Jewish Law. There they were, standing on the railway platform, together with the parents of one of them; the parents of the other had already been deported. Several men were holding an old prayer shawl over the pair. A few psalms were chanted, and the rabbi spoke a few words to them. Then he blessed them and they put their signatures to a scrap of paper. Now they were lawfully married. He gave them a final blessing and declared them man and wife – in life and in death.

And out there was the cattle truck – waiting.

CHAPTER 13

'Operation Embellishment'

One day there was a tremendous uproar in the camp. The cause, it seemed, was 'Operation Embellishment', though we had no idea what this could possibly mean. Later it emerged that Hitler wished to demonstrate to the world that in Theresienstadt he had created for the Jews a model state.

In the market square, where the three gallows had stood on which those young Czechs had been hanged as punishment for smuggling letters out of the camp, grass was now sown – what's more, it was Danish grass! We were puzzled that everything had become green in the short space of a fortnight. We resented the fact that the grass had come from Denmark. Tables and benches were placed in the market square. All of a sudden we were issued with new clothing and given a pot plant with paper flowers. We, who would not previously have been allowed to touch a blade of grass had we been able to find one, suddenly had a flowerpot in our room and pictures on the walls – idyllic scenes taken from magazines.

Something was afoot, but we did not know what it might be. Our guess was that there was going to be an inspection of the camp. Many of us believed that the inspectors might be Danes, and our hopes began to rise. We are not forgotten, we thought, someone remembers us. We were ordered to clean the streets – and not just the streets but also the pavements and the pathways, which were particularly filthy. We were given proper rags and real buckets with water; as a rule we had to beg for cleansing materials to enable us to clean our floors. That was in any case a hopeless task, as the centuries-old floorboards were encrusted with grime and full of fleas and other vermin.

Now we were on our knees in the street, scrubbing. The hearses were banished and hidden away. Strangers were not to see hearses laden alternately with bread and corpses. The houses were painted and a children's nursery set up, with bright blue and red beds. A well-known Dutch painter, Joe Spier, was instructed to paint cheerful murals. We knew, of course, that paint was scarce in Germany, but suddenly it appeared from nowhere and everything was given a fresh coat, but only in certain areas of the town; the rest was left in its usual state of squalor and decay.

One evening the order was given that a certain number of Danes were to leave their quarters. Some were to be housed in the lofts, others were to be sent out of the camp. Among the latter was Judge Moritz with whom we had been sharing our accommodation. There was no doubt that if a Danish commission were to come, Judge Moritz would not keep his mouth shut. He was so overwhelmed by a sense of the injustice to which he had been subjected that he would not consider the consequences of telling the truth. Just like Mrs Schultz and so many others who had lost relations in the camp, he had to be hidden away.

On the eve of the Danish Red Cross Commission's arrival, my husband, along with Dr Max Friediger, the Chief Rabbi of Copenhagen, and engineer Ove Meyer, were instructed to address the Danish inmates in the camp. They were to inform them of the consequences they would suffer if they gave anything away or if complaints and criticisms in any shape or form were uttered.

On 23 June 1944, the commission arrived; it consisted of

Franz Hvass, the top civil servant at the Danish Foreign Ministry, and E. Juel-Henningsen, the head physician at the Ministry of Health.

Dr Paul Eppstein had to act as mayor. He was issued with a dark pinstripe suit and an antiquated motor car. An SS man in civvies played the chauffeur – to Eppstein, the prisoner! This needed to appear impressive since Eppstein, together with the SS officers, had to accompany the Danish commission on a totally predetermined tour of the camp. He had to answer the questions put to him and report that there existed a school and a library and even a bank; and he had to describe the functions of the various 'institutions' positively, as instructed by the SS commandant.

Indeed, there was a bank, a real bank. The prisoners had, in the course of time, been sent money from all over the world, from relatives in England, Holland and Portugal, from Switzerland and from Sweden. In the world at large it was believed that in Theresienstadt one could buy anything for money, be it food or whatever else was needed.

We were issued with paper money, but what were we to do with it? Some notes were printed in-house, 'Moses-Scheine' as I called them. They showed a picture of Moses holding the two tablets with the Ten Commandments. There were units to the value of ten kronen, one hundred kronen, etc. That is what the Germans gave us, while retaining the real money for themselves. But it all looked like the genuine banking facilities of a normal country. And that was what the commission was shown. The gentlemen did not see the actual banknotes, but they saw that there was a bank with a counter and a till; they saw a ledger and savings books. People were paid 'wages' for their work, but the banknotes were worthless, since there was nothing to buy except used combs and old coat hangers. The money came in handy to light fires whenever we managed to get hold of some firewood or to plug our windows to prevent draughts. How could any reasonably sane person living in the real world ever guess that this was all one gigantic bluff?

For this special occasion shop-windows had been mocked-up, displaying meat and sausages and fresh vegetables – things we had not seen since we were incarcerated. There was food in great abundance, as proof that we could buy anything we needed. The captives were completely overcome by the sight of all that meat, having had none at all for ages.

The gentlemen of the commission were shown that cornucopia. They were meant to see that we had 'shops' where we could make purchases. They were shown 'evidence' that we had enough to eat. Our rations were temporarily three times their usual size and of a totally different quality. The visitors were present to watch the inmates collect these extra rations.

The very old and those of sickly appearance had either been removed or locked up in their quarters, while the younger ones and the women were displayed; the latter had – as a consequence of the conditions in the camp, the anxieties and the undernourishment – ceased to menstruate and had become very bloated. That gave them the appearance of well-fed people. The two gentlemen were also shown the children who had just come from Czechoslovakia and were accordingly still in reasonably good shape.

All the people who had been employed on the embellishment of Theresienstadt before the commission's arrival were led to believe that, for the time being, they were safe from transportation. They were thanked by the Council of Elders who conveyed to them the commandant's official appreciation. The poor wretches, however, in thinking themselves secure from dispatch to a worse fate, were mistaken. They were nearly all taken away in a transport of seven thousand five hundred souls some time before the commission's arrival. They knew too much about the lies and chicanery; besides, Theresienstadt was on no account to appear overcrowded.

CHAPTER 14

Are the Commissioners Deceived?

I felt sure that the commission must have realised that all was not as it seemed. Where in Germany would so much paint be wasted at that time in order to colour buildings bright blue or red? And were the two gentlemen really taken in by those finely decked out beds for the little children? I was convinced they must have seen through it all. But how could they possibly have guessed at all the degradations people were exposed to in Theresienstadt?

How could they tell, for instance, that many were dying for want of medication, while deliveries of medicines kept arriving from abroad, most recently a large consignment from Switzerland? My husband was at that time summoned to the commandant's headquarters where, under duress, he was forced to sign a document stating that there was no shortage of medicines in the camp and that there were doctors and nurses treating the sick. The medicines were returned to Switzerland with the suggestion that they should be sent to regions where those remedies were really in short supply. My husband was often compelled to translate messages which had come from Denmark or Sweden. We were not allowed to receive letters, only postcards, and my husband had to declare on his honour that they contained nothing about the war or any other news which the commandant sought to withhold from us. If there were questions as to whether we were hungry or were short of anything we might want, then the cards would, of course, be destroyed. His was a dangerous job, because no one could prevent my husband from passing on any important news.

No hint of the truth must be conveyed to the two visitors as they were conducted on their tour. They had been placed among some Danish inmates who were under orders to tell them the official version of what was going on in the camp and how well we were faring. When asked what we needed, my husband did not quite know how to respond. He could not very well reply that we were in want of food, of freedom, of absolutely everything; that would have finished him as well as the rest of us. He said that we would like a few books. We had nothing to read in the camp other than some old, mainly theological, works written in Czech.

One particular nuisance was the presence of the accursed criminal investigation officer Renner of the German Security Police in Copenhagen. He had already been a spy in the camp of Horserød. He understood every word of Danish. We could not even talk in whispers to the emissaries because that gangster officer was always nearby. From his time at Camp Horserød he knew everyone's identity and, of course, here too he had his Gestapo spies. One always had to be aware that in a camp of forty thousand people there would be spies. None of us knew who they were, but how else could so much of what people were talking about reach the Nazis' ears?

When Franz Hvass and Juel-Henningsen left the house where they had exchanged a few words with the three Danes (Ove Meyer, Chief Rabbi Max Friediger and my husband), they proceeded to the newly created kindergarten where they were to be shown how well the children were being cared for. My daughter who was working in the kindergarten was determined somehow to make contact with the commission, but she knew that, as they were surrounded by SS officers, a direct approach to the guests would be impossible. Accordingly, she had used bits of her mattress (a sack of straw) to sew a belt for herself and had borrowed a few coloured crayons from the children. Those children who had come from Prague had been permitted to bring along a few of their things, including toys. With the help of their crayons she painted the colours of the Danish flag on her belt, wound it round her waist, and hoped the commission would recognise her as a Dane. When she was standing close by Juel-Henningsen she picked up a child in her arms and gave it a little pinch on the leg to make it cry; she then tried to whisper to Juel-Henningsen the word 'hunger' and also, 'Give my regards to Dr Per Thygesen in Copenhagen.' Per Thygesen never received that message from Juel-Henningsen who had evidently not taken it in.

On that day the children were given a little more food, some sweetish cakes, I believe. They were in their seventh heaven. I keep thinking about those children, running about the camp. Most of them were alone, without any family; their parents had been taken from them and deported from Theresienstadt to 'other camps'. Many of the adult inmates made a serious attempt to take care of those waifs. The Danish children, for example, were given clandestine lessons (in so far as this was possible) by some young women who had been halfway through their teacher-training before they were sent to the camp. We also tried to bring together the Czech, Austrian and German children, but some of them were completely lost to normal society and had become wild and aggressive. They were profoundly unhappy and did not know which way to turn. As a rule the children received somewhat better food than the adults; that was something we had finally achieved with the commandant.

On the occasion of the inspection a sign had been affixed to the door of the bogus school with the message: SCHOOL FOR GIRLS AND BOYS *Closed for the holidays*. When the commission was inspecting the newly refurbished children's home, the repulsive SS Commandant Karl Rahm placed himself in full view, legs apart and arms akimbo. Presently one of the children, obedient to instructions, ran up to him, hugged him and cried out: 'Hi, uncle, are you coming to play with us? What have you brought us today?' On that day the children were given bread and sardines. They had been instructed to throw the food to the ground the moment the commission was approaching. They were to make a fuss and shout: 'What? Do we have to eat sardines *again*?' Few of them actually knew what sardines were, but the performance had been well rehearsed and went off splendidly.

And the gentlemen of the Danish commission had to watch and listen to this charade arranged in their honour.

CHAPTER 15

Aftermath of the Visit

One thing the two Danish visitors must surely have become aware of: Eppstein was not allowed to sit down. He had to stand the whole time, even when all the others were seated. On the other hand, it might just as easily have escaped their attention – it is hard to say. No decent Dane – and, of course, both of them were decent – could have seen through all the falsehood and deceit in the course of a few hours when all they were shown was what the Germans intended them to see. Even if they had been able to sense that there was something going on which was being deliberately hidden from them, they could not possibly have guessed at the full horror.

How could any civilised person begin to imagine the diabolical schemes the Nazis had devised? How could anyone know that the Germans had already drawn up plans to rid themselves of all the Theresienstadt prisoners? Those plans were to be set in motion when the end of the war was in sight. The Germans knew full well that one fine day the Russians would conquer Theresienstadt, but before that day came they would finish us all off. My husband had recorded in a small notebook (which is still in my possession) that Eppstein had told him about gas-chambers which had been built in the crematorium to kill inmates.

Alas, we had been sorely deluding ourselves with the insane hope that the commission's visit would have a positive effect and would lead to an improvement in our situation. The members of the commission had seen that splendid green market square with tables and chairs where people were sitting. But they had not seen that all their coffee cups were empty. They had walked about and talked to people now and then. But since we had all been strictly forbidden to give anything away, the commissioners were completely fooled and had no means of penetrating the web of intrigue and make-believe.

Had they discovered the truth, I do not know how much hotter our hell would have been made by the Nazis. In the event, it may have been to our advantage that the members of the commission could only report what they had actually seen but not understood.

After their departure it was back to the old conditions. The flowerpots were taken away, as was the special issue of clothing. Our rations became even smaller than before; meat and sausages vanished from the shop-windows the same day and found their way back to the German command. The aim had been to convince the members of the commission that there were ample supplies in the camp, readily available for purchase whenever people fancied them – even though in Germany itself food was rationed. I do not know whether the commissioners found this fact perplexing.

Among the matters of which the commission remained in ignorance was the fate of the so-called mayor, Paul Eppstein. Shortly after their departure he had a word with my husband who, he assumed, must have known the Danish members of the commission. Eppstein wanted to know what, in my husband's opinion, their impression might have been; did he think they had seen through that farce?

Eppstein was in utter despair. He called himself 'mayor by remote control'. He was deeply unhappy that he had not been able to communicate anything, not even by insinuation: 'Do I not know what is happening to people here? Do I not know what happens to them when they are deported?' I shall never forget that. His wife was terribly dejected, tears running down her face. For her the visit – with all the preparations and all the deceit in which she had been compelled to take part – had proved an unbearable trial.

Two days later Eppstein was taken away, to the little fortress beyond the camp where he was brutally tortured and murdered. He knew too much. A short while later his wife was dispatched to one of the extermination camps. I saw her leave, together with a friend whose whole body was covered in cancerous sores and bandaged from top to toe. Mrs Eppstein told me that she was really proud to be following her husband.

That is how it was. I shall never forget it.

How could the commissioners have had the faintest suspicion what the consequences of their visit would be?

CHAPTER 16

The Propaganda Film

To demonstrate what a good life we were leading in this model camp – as the Germans dubbed Theresienstadt – a film was to be made about this marvellous place.

One of the inmates, Kurt Gerron, who had been a film director of repute in Berlin, was to direct the film. We were seated at tables, set with cups and paper flowers, while some well-known artists performed themes from musicals. My husband and I were placed at a table in a far corner, and so we were hopeful that we would not be visible in the film. There was a large stage on which a few women in low-cut dresses appeared, and there was a male choir dressed in what looked like tails. The musicians with their instruments were seated in the orchestra pit; the more famous among them were to be shown off. Spotlights were erected in large numbers, and the whole thing was rigorously supervised by SS men who were placed everywhere.

Then the farce began. We were to pretend we were drinking from the empty cups and having animated conversations. The music started with a Viennese waltz, and the people had to dance – they were made to dance and to sing! But their sad eyes could not be hidden away so easily.

I do not believe that the film was widely distributed, for the war was drawing to a close and there would not have been time – much to the Nazis' regret, no doubt – to let this film tell the world of our wonderful life in Theresienstadt. This wicked web of lies was introduced by a speaker with the following words: 'While the Jews in Theresienstadt are sitting in cafés, enjoying themselves over coffee and cakes, dancing and singing, our own German citizens are having to bear the gravest burdens of this terrible war, to suffer misery and privation in order to save the fatherland.'

Yes, that was some propaganda.

The director, Kurt Gerron, was subsequently sent off to 'other work', in Nazi terminology, namely the gas chamber. He had been toiling day and night in the hope that by his tireless efforts he might escape deportation. At the same time, he was aware that few got away with their lives once they knew the truth about the campaign of deceit and the catalogue of crimes against humanity. He was removed – and this was the fate shared by many of the musicians and singers, as well as the thousands of extras who had been forced to take part in the crowd scenes of the film.

CHAPTER 17

Mass Deportation of Children

Six months after the Danish Red Cross Commissioners visited Theresienstadt nearly all the children who had been present during the 'embellishment' activities were deported – the very children who had been playing and gambolling in front of the commissioners. The same fate was meted out to the youngsters who had taken part in the propaganda film which had been made in connection with the embellishment effort.

We knew many of the children who were removed; some of the Czech ones we knew particularly well. Whenever a parcel arrived for us and my husband went to fetch it, one boy called Frantisek would closely follow him. Sometimes there were lollipops or other sweets in the packet. I must admit that we ourselves had a great craving for sweets. All the same, my husband could not help giving him some. By and by children were sticking to him like flies.

On one occasion my elder son sent a few oranges from Sweden. I think there were six. Frantisek and the other children caught a glimpse of them; they had never before seen an orange. Even before they were taken to a concentration camp, Jewish children in occupied countries had been forbidden to eat tropical fruit. Their parents had not been allowed to buy such luxuries. Another time there were two lemons in a parcel. Goodness knows, many of the children looked in desperate need of vitamins and I thought to myself: lemons contain vitamin C, don't they? So I cut up a lemon into eight slices which I distributed to the children. But the youngsters, never having tasted a lemon before, found them too bitter.

You could often observe children in Theresienstadt standing by the walls licking the chalk they contained. It is remarkable how nature helps itself: suddenly masses of children would be licking the walls and the iron gates to obtain in this way some of the nutrients which they were short of.

On one occasion Miss Phillipson, the elder of our block, came to see me. She used to call in for a chat most evenings. She gave me a small triangular piece of linen which was the signal that I was to help with the transport the next day. When I arrived, I found the railway station and the whole surrounding area teeming with children. My heart nearly stopped when I saw that. There were tiny little children alongside the older ones. It was a totally numbing sight. Hardly any of them spoke; hardly any of them even cried. They stood there staring. But the SS guards were in a jolly mood. One girl turned to me and said: 'Now we are allowed to go home.' Another was doubtful and asked me: 'But are we really, do you think?'

What was in store for these children? An extermination camp, and no chance of survival. One was standing here and one could do nothing. What would have become of those children had they been allowed to grow up in ordinary circumstances and lead a normal life? No doubt many among them were gifted and highly intelligent youngsters. They would have achieved a lot and enriched the world! A whole generation was being wiped out. One felt choked and short of breath watching them being pushed into the cattle trucks. Some were looking out and waved as the doors were slammed shut. Many seemed to have a premonition of what was to happen to them – it could be seen in their eyes.

Frantisek, the boy who had never before seen an orange, was among the children who were sent to their death on that fateful day in September 1944 when the 'Kindertransport' left Theresienstadt. The commands rang out. I helped Frantisek with his rucksack. I could not speak. He put his arms round my neck, his eyes full of tears. Did he sense that we would never see each other again? Then he marched off with all the other children, big and small. Some of them were so tiny that they had to be carried by the older ones. We heard the shouts of the Gestapo and the baying of the hounds; not a sound from the children. I asked myself: are they human beings, these Nazis? Are they really capable of cramming all those children into cattle wagons as if they were so many packages?

We were ordered off the platform. Svend Meyer – one of the few Danes doing transport duty – and I looked at each other. We could not speak. If only Eppstein had never hinted at what awaited those who were being dispatched from here! If only one could close one's mind as one could shut one's mouth and eyes. Was that really me who was living through that nightmare?! Would anyone in Denmark – should we ever get home – believe what we had witnessed today? Svend Meyer was sobbing. He at least might find relief in tears. And so fifteen thousand children vanished from Theresienstadt.

What could the world be doing? Had the Danish Red Cross Commissioners really had no inkling of the horrors? Surely they must have known that they had not just come here in honour of us Danes, but that they bore responsibility also for the others. In the light of the total catastrophe we were quite insignificant. We were, after all, relatively few – compared with the thousands who were being deported and exterminated. If only the commission had seen through some of the deception, they could have passed on their impressions overseas through secret channels. That had been our hope.

However, what really happened in Theresienstadt (and indeed elsewhere) was only made public after the war had ended.

CHAPTER 18

Continuing Hunger

Time was passing and people were losing all hope. Some shut their eyes and vegetated from day to day; a few died. In the course of time, a few babies were born, but none survived more than a day or two. Only those babies whose mothers had been pregnant on arrival in Theresienstadt were allowed to be born. Otherwise parents and doctors in the camp were forbidden on pain of death to bring children into the world. In any event, how could mothers feed their babies on a diet of soup made of potato peelings? They would have died of lack of nourishment.

At the same time, I have to mention – and this sounds quite appalling – that hunger drives people to acts of the most unbelievable nature. I saw mothers of three- to four-year olds fetch their children's food and, unable to resist the temptation, help themselves to some of the soup meant for the infants. They did so despite their love for their children. Extreme hunger can drive human beings to inhuman behaviour. On the other hand, there were of course many mothers, indeed the majority, who made immense sacrifices for the good of their children.

Every block in the camp received a certain allocation of bread which had to be shared out, half a loaf per inmate per week. But that did not mean that the four of us received two whole loaves between us – not at all. The woman in charge of our block used to cut each loaf in half and take a slice of each half for herself. We asked her many times why we could not have two whole loaves and divide them ourselves, but she would not agree – she insisted on her share. We simply had to submit to this, for in a place where many were capable of anything just to survive, normal rules of civilised life did not apply.

Sometimes we even had squabbles with our own children. We often tried to give them an extra piece of our own bread, but they would not take it; it would go back and forth between us and no one would give way. Eventually a solution would be found.

Vegetables were not obtainable in the camp. I remember one occasion when a Czech lady gave us four chives, one for each member of our family. And I recall an old German Jewish surgeon who would always be summoned to the Nazi barracks to treat SS people when they were taken ill. For such duties he was reckoned to be good enough. On his return he often brought back a handful of grass which he had plucked outside the camp. He would use that grass for its vitamins and eat it with his soup. We all had mighty cravings for anything green.

Apropos of the bread – I am reminded of something relating to Judge Moritz and his sister. My son had contracted polio and was paralysed. He was taken into quarantine where he was crammed in with people suffering from diphtheria, scarlet fever and heaven knows what. They were housed in the very prison cell where Gavrilo Princip, the assassin of Archduke Franz Ferdinand of Austria, had been held prisoner. There my son lay. To begin with, there were still some doctors and nurses, but in time they were deported. There had been one transport consisting exclusively of people who had been concerned with healthcare. Somehow my son survived, but when he came back after several months, there was not much left of him and he could barely walk. Needless to say, the sick received no more food than the rest of us. Well, Judge Moritz and his sister had woven a long cord out of the straw of their mattress and tied to it a piece of bread which they had then squeezed through the cracks in the floorboards to reach my son lying down below in the cellar. That was a tremendous act of generosity whose value no one can appreciate who has not lived and starved in a Nazi camp.

These people were so utterly selfless, even though, like everyone else, they were hard pressed to get hold of something edible. But they remained steadfast and staunch in the face of those abominable conditions. We have never forgotten their generosity. Poor Judge Moritz died two days before we returned home: he died of leukaemia and hunger and homesickness. Thoughts about Denmark and pining for the past had occupied his mind from morning until night, day after day. Eventually he did come home – after the end of the war – but only as ashes.

CHAPTER 19

Lack of Medication

One of my companions was a doctor from Czechoslovakia, a very competent and sensible lady who was full of goodness and humanity. We had many conversations, for my son was working as her medical assistant. Indeed, it was this doctor who had diagnosed his polio.

She was working in a hospital dating back to the time of Maria Theresa; alas, there was only the most primitive equipment and no medicines at all. Whenever any top Nazis were taken ill, they would suddenly remember that there were excellent doctors among the inmates and they would consult them, quite ignoring the fact that they were Jews. Any necessary medicaments and instruments would miraculously be procured. If the outcome was satisfactory no thanks were offered. But heaven help the doctor if anything went awry. Eventually the SS people would even bring their families to Theresienstadt to be treated by an eminent ophthalmologist whom they were holding prisoner there.

I remember that Willie Levysohn from Copenhagen became seriously ill. He was a robust middle-aged man who was assigned to pulling the vehicles carrying coal for command headquarters. Horses were reckoned to be too precious for that labour, whereas humans were highly expendable. In Copenhagen, Levysohn had led a comfortable life and had, among other things, been a member of the Chamber of

Commercial and Maritime Law. At his age, suffering as he was from diabetes, he was bound to find hard labour unendurable and visibly caved in. There was no insulin or other therapeutic remedy; we requested Gertrud Adler, the Czech doctor, to help him in whatever way she could, but there was nothing at all that she could do. My husband comforted him with the thought that an ambulance from Denmark would soon be on its way to fetch him home. I think he died without realising how very ill he was. To the last he kept asking why the ambulance from home had not yet arrived. Many of our other Danish friends also died, most of them from hunger and from lack of medication.

One day when I arrived for duty at one of the transportations, I spotted Dr Adler with her nice mother of whom she was exceedingly fond. The old lady had been selected for deportation, and her daughter had volunteered to go with her – despite her mother's entreaty to her to stay behind in Theresienstadt where her husband was interned as well. When I saw those two standing on the platform, suitcase in hand, I thought how it might have been a railway station anywhere – in Italy or in England – they looked so calm and collected. No doubt they had a pretty shrewd idea that they were going to their death, but they were determined to keep their fear concealed. Serenely they climbed from the platform on to the cattle truck and were gone. We never heard from them again.

On rare occasions some of the Germans who had been treated by Jewish doctors in the camp would leave remnants of their medicines behind. In normal circumstances such things would be shared out for the benefit of all those who were sick. Here, however, one had to beg or bribe with bread or other food or curry favour with friends and acquaintances. That was the way it was, and people were becoming accustomed to this state of affairs. Moral concepts had lost their real meaning.

In this travesty of a town, we were carrying on a parody of

normal life. It seemed as though all notions of value were transformed – for the Danes as well as the rest of the forty thousand prisoners. The borderline between right and wrong became blurred to fit the conditions to which people were exposed. I doubt that anyone nowadays, born and bred in a constitutional state where the rule of law prevails, could comprehend what the inmates of Theresienstadt were driven to.

Such a situation spelled great danger, especially for children. They were growing up thieves and liars in order to stay alive. They had never experienced anything else, and many of them had seen their parents vanish from the camp without trace. What would become of them later on in the world outside after they were released – those few hundred who might survive? What could they know of moral rectitude? How would they manage to find their way to a normal existence after all they had been through?

CHAPTER 20

Adapting to the System

Hunger remained our main preoccupation and occasionally led to the strangest events. Engineer Ove Meyer suffered dreadfully from hunger. By chance he made the acquaintance of a Dutch lady who had previously worked for Radio Amsterdam. She was one of the few from Holland not to have been deported before; most of her fellow-Jews had ended up in Auschwitz.

She was employed in the so-called soup kitchen where she could get food and was, therefore, not in need of her own rations. She and Meyer came to an agreement whereby he would get her rations and she was to note down every single date on which he had obtained her portion. In the event of their survival, he undertook to pay her a princely sum for each and every meal he had had. My husband, who was a lawyer, drew up a proper contract which was signed by witnesses. He as well as both parties received a copy to which they put their signatures. Fortunately both of them regained their freedom and in 1945 the Dutch lady came to Denmark and, in the presence of my husband, received the sum which Ove Meyer owed her.

Of course, the additional food was of enormous benefit to Ove Meyer. At the front of everyone's mind was the overwhelming problem of hunger and the craving for food. Some people became quite aggressive and there would occur the most extraordinary outbursts. When Austrians and Czechs happened to meet, they would often become very unpleasant and get under each other's skin, just because hunger had made them so irritable. The Czechs would charge the Austrian inmates with responsibility for Austria's subjugation of Czechoslovakia. Yet those poor prisoners in the concentration camp could surely not be blamed for the conquest of Bohemia or for Austria's having started the First World War in 1914. The Austrian Jews accused the German Jews of being 'Oh, so German', but in fact the two groups were quarrelling because they were exasperated and needed to let off steam.

Certain people served in the higher echelons of the Jewish self-administration of the camp. It was likely that they obtained more to eat than the others and they clearly enjoyed privileged status. Each nation had its own spokesman; the Danes were represented by Chief Rabbi Dr Max Friediger. Those representatives had some influence on the running of affairs. There was a great difference between them and the ordinary prisoners. They had a certain status and could make decisions affecting others.

The first arrivals in Theresienstadt, the Czechs, had of course taken charge of the best available jobs, such as the soup kitchen, the distribution of food, in fact anything connected with catering. When the Danes arrived at the camp, in October 1943, they were given the worst and most arduous type of work as well as the smallest rations. One of the inmates, who had been in the camp for several years, pointed out that he and his fellows had been there when the Danes were still living at home in their own country in comfort and with excellent food.

The abrupt exposure to life in a concentration camp had a terrible effect on many Danes, especially in the early stages; they became emaciated, wasted away, and some died – like, for example, our lawyer friend Axel Metz from Odense.

Some of them sank into deepest depression and became totally passive. They saw nothing, they heard nothing and they moved about as in a dream. No wonder they could not adjust to their new situation. Having lost all interest in their fellow creatures, they eventually lost interest in themselves.

There were a few people who had formerly led a hard life, labouring for low wages before being taken to Theresienstadt from Austria, Czechoslovakia, Germany or Holland. By and large they had greater stamina and were better able to cope with the terrible conditions than those who had come from a more privileged background. For those who had been leading more sheltered lives the transition was exceedingly tough. But there were no hard and fast rules, much depended on strength of character, self-discipline and the individual will to hold out. What was remarkable was how people perceived themselves once they were interned in the camp. Several of the Czechs had been miners working in the big Bohemian mines. When they were asked what they had done before in their normal life, the answer invariably was that they had been mine owners. It was not unusual for people to romanticise and gild the past in order to impress their fellow-inmates and indeed themselves.

Having been torn from normal life and plunged into that nightmare existence, people became nostalgic about the past, tending to embroider it and view it through rose-tinted spectacles. It helped them rise above the never-ending desolation and anonymity of their present situation. Fantasising is plainly a natural psychological phenomenon, an understandable type of escapism when faced with the absurdity and abnormality of life prevailing in a concentration camp. Our existence could not really be called life but a mere semblance of life which is impossible to describe to those who have not actually experienced such conditions.

Yet, how was it that there were relatively few suicides? Was it the instinct for self-preservation? Was it hope? Did fathers and mothers shrink from taking such steps for fear of abandoning the children they had brought into the world? Or was it that people were too drained of strength and willpower to determine their own destiny?

CHAPTER 21

Lottery of Deportation

Meanwhile the transportations were continuing without remission; there were arrivals and there were departures. At the Nazis' insistence the internal administration of the camp was run by the Jews themselves. The SS commandant issued daily orders which had to be obeyed to the letter, point by point. SS messengers would deliver lists to the Council of Elders detailing the categories of prisoners to be deported. As a rule they would arrive in the middle of the night without any prior warning. The house elder in each block had to see to it that orders were carried out and that the victims were notified at what time and at what barracks they were to report, regardless of whether they were capable of walking or needed to be carried. The prisoners themselves received a note with their names and transport numbers.

Unfortunately, many families – husbands, wives, children – were housed long distances from each other. But gradually some had managed to move in together in secret. Most of them, however, had to live apart and were subject to curfew at the onset of dark. So, if the notifications arrived in the evening or at night, spouses were invariably unable to communicate with each other or with their families. And early next morning they had to present themselves at the 'channel'. That was the place for them to assemble prior to being loaded into the transport wagons.

Often they would have to linger in the 'channel' for a day or two before the departure of the trains. But, once they were there, they were no longer allowed to make contact with their families. They could only communicate via those who had been ordered to assist with the children and the sick and the old who could not fend for themselves. Of these, some could barely move and were lying on the ground already near death.

Sometimes the Germans demanded that seven thousand people be deported at one fell swoop; other times it was five thousand. Altogether about ninety thousand were deported from Theresienstadt; approximately thirty-five thousand met their death in the camp; and only around eleven thousand remained alive when the camp was liberated in 1945.

Sometimes those designated for deportation would, on receipt of their transport order, rush to the building where the Council of Elders was assembled and attempt to gain exemption from deportation. There invariably were some who knew one or other of the elders. Several of them would try to buy their freedom with, for instance, a piece of jewellery which on arrival they had managed to smuggle into the camp and which they had somehow kept concealed. If they succeeded in their bid for exemption, any inmate who happened to be standing around in the street might simply be picked up at random and dispatched instead. After all, the SS did not care one way or another which person the elders included. Their main concern was that the figures should add up and that the specified numbers from the designated groups should be ready for deportation.

I don't quite know what to call the elders' behaviour – 'corruption' perhaps? However inexcusable, it was perfectly understandable that they should try to prevent their own relatives and friends from being dispatched. In fact, the Germans compelled the hapless people in charge to become the executioners of their brothers by having to make life and death decisions. In this way people's characters inevitably underwent change. For one could not be at the apex of the camp organisation without submitting to the system. At times misuse of power was forced upon those who were in a position to help their nearest and dearest. And how many would not have done the same in such dire circumstances? Did that make them worse than all the others? Were they worse than those who stole bread from the old, the sick and the blind? Indeed, there were a few who did just that, people whose hunger and fear of dying had robbed them of their last scruples.

Why did we not protest when we saw someone being snatched without warning for deportation? Such a person would be picked up arbitrarily – and whisked away to the cattle truck! Knowing we were powerless to prevent such things, we just stood there and looked on. We were as helpless as the one who was plucked at random.

It was a kind of power game. Some of those at the top were trying to maintain their positions and to make themselves indispensable in Theresienstadt. There would be squabbles and intrigues; it is understandable that under such conditions people did not become any better or more considerate. There were good human beings and bad ones – just as in any other society. However, in the prevailing conditions people's characteristics became more pronounced owing to the pressures from above as well as from below. How were they to conduct themselves? The cunning one always gets the better of the less cunning – and so it was in Theresienstadt.

CHAPTER 22

Destroying the Evidence

Suddenly all transports from Theresienstadt ceased because, it was said, the Russians were approaching. From that moment, the Germans were busy wiping out all traces of their evil-doing.

Until then the cardboard boxes containing the ashes of deceased inmates had been stacked in one place and labelled with names. Now they were being thrown into the river, and ten- to twelve-year-old children, of all people, were charged with this job. There was a little Danish boy whose surname was noticed by another boy on one of the cardboard boxes. He said to the child: 'Look, this is the same name as yours.' In fact it was the father of the little boy, who had died a short while before, and now the children had to throw his ashes into the river. Theresienstadt children were hardened at an early age.

The Germans were now burning their archives. Old Mrs Schultz, in her eighty-fourth year, would climb up to a window facing the barracks where the archives were stored – dossiers from the secret police in Berlin and documentation about everything that had occurred in Theresienstadt. The Germans had kept detailed records of captives, deportations, deaths, rations, forced labour, production, etc. The Nazis had not expected the camp to be bombed by the Allies because that would put the inmates at risk; they had therefore considered Theresienstadt to be a safe place for storing their archives.

Now Mrs Schultz could see the Nazis burning huge bundles of archive material – consigning more and more paper to the flames. The inmates were strictly forbidden to look out of the windows, but Mrs Schultz, that nimble little person, would clamber up regardless and observe what was going on. From time to time she would jump up and down excitedly and exclaim that now they were redoubling their efforts. That surely meant that the war must be drawing to a close.

The Nazis did not, however, manage to destroy everything. Many papers were later found by the Czechs: files and dossiers recording what had happened in Theresienstadt. Thus the Nazis' deeds could be documented in the perpetrators' own words. The Czechs also found large numbers of drawings and sketches left behind by deportees, among whom there had been many gifted artists from several countries, but chiefly from Czechoslovakia and the Netherlands. Altogether they presented an unvarnished picture of life in Theresienstadt.

The artists had depicted daily existence in a concentration camp, with all its agonies and torments; they had intended their sketches to bear witness to the endless mean and vile acts to which they and their fellow inmates had been subjected. But some of the hidden sketches had been discovered by the SS, and the artists who had been trying to tell the truth paid for it with their lives. Nevertheless, a few of the deported painters had been successful in hiding some of their pictures in a wall cavity, and there they were found after the war.

Also sketches by children, which survived their young creators, tell about their lives and the images which had remained in their memories: drawings of parents, of houses in which they had once been happy, of cats, dogs and horses they had loved in the past. They depicted their friends on bunks and men on gallows, cattle trucks as well as long queues of the starving.

CHAPTER 23

Plans for the 'Final Solution'

At the beginning of 1945 a transport from Eastern Europe arrived in Theresienstadt. It brought Hungarians who had been evacuated from another concentration camp. They were crawling with lice, and it was my lot to be among the delousers. The delousing centre was a terrible room where people, having been stripped of their clothes, were shaved of every single hair. They were then disinfected in some corrosive solution which damaged the hands. Many of those undergoing this process of delousing were, as a consequence, taken seriously ill; indeed there were quite a number of deaths. Others arrived in camp suffering from typhoid fever, so that prisoners who might have survived the defeat of the Nazis lost their lives at the last moment.

One day in February 1945 my husband came back from work in the environment administration department looking deathly pale. His colleague at work was the Czech engineer Erich Kohn who was constantly being summoned to the Gestapo commandant to receive orders for the so-called 'internal administration'. On that February day, Kohn had been called to the terrain outside the moat. There he found Karl Rahm, the commandant, and several SS officers. They told him that it was intended to establish a new 'channel' at this point.

The moat dating back to the time of Maria Theresa was

surrounded by some sort of bulwark. The River Eger which ran close by Theresienstadt was to be channelled into the moat. There was only one exit out of that fortress down to the water. Once that was shut off no one could ever escape from it. Engineer Kohn along with other engineers received orders to join up the bulwarks. The Germans had worked out precisely how that was to be done. The plan was to create a huge duck pond, they said. But the engineers became suspicious. They had a foreboding of some catastrophe when they overheard a conversation between the commandant and his deputy. Suddenly it became clear to them that all the captives in Theresienstadt were to be lured into that trap, perhaps on the pretext of a census, such as we had experienced on that gruesome day, 11 November 1943, out on the field. When all the thousands of people had been assembled down in the channel, the sluicegates would be opened, releasing floods of water which would engulf them all. If anyone should attempt to escape, the soldiers stationed up on the walls would be ready for them with flame-throwers.

Everyone working in the environment department, including my husband, was to start immediately noting down yet again the numbers of all the prisoners (who had, of course, long before all been allocated numbers). And that was to be the end of it all. There was to be no exemption for the Danes, although we had heard that the King of Denmark had made great efforts to save our lives. But in a contest with the SS even a king was the loser. Now that Hitler and Himmler were doomed to failure, the Germans had to find a way out, for it must not be revealed that the people in Theresienstadt had been subject to forced labour and had been starved to death. After all, it had supposedly been a 'model camp'.

It was by some miracle that in the end the Nazis were unable to put their diabolical plan into action. The Russians were approaching and the Gestapo and SS were busy taking care of the security of their documents and indeed of their own safety. It was most fortunate that this horrendous scheme was overtaken by events and could no longer be carried out. The idea had been that on 10 May Theresienstadt would be rased to the ground, but their own defeat pre-empted the Nazis' implementation of that plan.

CHAPTER 24

Deliverance

One day in April 1945 a command was issued without any warning: we Danes were ordered into the casemates, leaving behind all our old rags; documents, papers, personal belongings, nothing was to be taken with us. But my husband succeeded in hiding his little notebook, and my son managed to conceal all the bits of paper on which he had recorded what had happened to him.

We were dispatched down to the casemates, underneath one of the barracks, where we were to await developments. We spent several days there. We did not dare hope that we might be going home, but Ove Meyer told us that he had seen a Swedish bus with his own eyes.

And now, at the very end, we saw things which we could not have imagined. Many of the young Danes had met and fallen in love with Czech and Austrian girls. And their farewells were heartrending. They were desperately clinging to each other, and knowing that it was goodbye forever and that they were unlikely to meet again, they did things in the presence of others which in normal life would have been unthinkable.

Well, it suddenly began to sink in: we were going home! We were mustered in columns and counted yet again. And then we saw a Swede, a real live Swede, wearing a Red Cross uniform – and without a machine gun. It was indescribable. We hardly dared show our joy but we understood that we might at any moment be collected and escorted away. Yet, what of all the others, all those we had come to know and who would be left behind, exposed to all the dangers? What fate was awaiting them? We feared for their safety. What if the SS carried out their fiendish intention to drown the remaining captives in the 'duck pond'?

No, we could not rejoice.

I think that must sound very peculiar. After all, it would have been quite natural for us to be jubilant. But no one felt that way, for we were filled with foreboding that those remaining behind might have a poor chance of survival. We knew little about the general theatre of war and whether the end was really in sight.

And yet we were leaving Theresienstadt. There were the white buses awaiting us. We could not believe our eyes.

Then all the inmates came to say goodbye to us, those dear people who had to stay put, all those who were not Danes. We were fortunate, however, to be allowed to take with us the German, Austrian and Czech refugee children whom we had brought to Denmark before the war. The Danish Government had granted them Danish citizenship.

So we climbed into the buses, where we met the chief physician Carl Krebs as well as Danish and Swedish members of the Red Cross. We were to depart at once on account of the massive bombing of Dresden which had just taken place, and it was feared that the roads might become impassable. The windows of the bus had to be kept closed and the curtains drawn. We were not to see what was going on outside; the German liaison officer who was travelling with us saw to that.

We reached Potsdam just after an air attack on the town, and our journey was halted. We were totally exhausted. In one of the suburbs we left the bus and sat down on the grass. For the first time since deportation we were able to relax in a real meadow. We could hear aircraft flying over the city and the sound of bombs exploding. But, to be honest, we were not much concerned. Yes, we heard the bombs drop, but we had just been rescued from Theresienstadt, and a bombardment was not really a big deal! At least, we had got away.

We saw people passing, small boys who had been stuffed into uniforms and who were expected to confront the approaching enemy. We also saw German fugitives hastening past. The Russians could not be far away.

We were all very weary and, at the same time, elated at the thought that the nightmare was nearing its end. There was no time to pause for food, we had to journey on. Finally we got to Padborg and at long last the bus driver could stop for a short while. Quite spontaneously, many of the town's citizens came out and invited us into their homes. And there were real washbasins and real soap. I could not get over it: I glanced down and saw a clean and polished floor; I lay in a real bed with real eiderdowns. It was like a fantastic adventure. And the people brought us flowers and chocolate and sandwiches. Some of our group fell upon all those goodies but, not being used to such rich food, became quite sick from over-indulgence.

Our journey continued via Fyn, where the Germans had organised an air-raid alarm to prevent any inhabitants on the street from seeing the white buses and demonstrating.

When we reached Copenhagen we were not allowed to stay there. We had to take the ferry to Sweden. That is where our adventure came to an end – but not before we had been through quarantine. We were suspected of carrying typhoid germs since most of us had been suffering from the disease to a greater or lesser extent.

The people were exceptionally friendly and helpful, and many Danes had made the journey to Malmö to welcome us. Unsurprisingly, there were those among them who failed to grasp what we were trying briefly to recount. After all, they thought, we had been released, so it could not have been that bad. The main thing, surely, was that we were now back home. Many of them did exclaim how absolutely ghastly we were looking, just like corpses. Why, they wondered, did we have such a deathly appearance? How were we to respond? Where to start and where to finish? We were perfectly aware that in their wildest imaginings they could never have envisaged what we had suffered. I have asked myself many times since then whether it was really me who experienced that hell – and if so, how I could ever have come through it?

Yet, consider what is going on in many parts of the world to this very day, and how people are being persecuted! However many food parcels we may send to refugee centres and prison camps in Africa or elsewhere, our experience tells us that the poor victims may never receive the food at all; it may well be stolen *en route*. Nevertheless, even if it is plundered – just as our food was plundered – there is always some hope that a few spoonfuls of rice might get through to those who are starving.

For today, once again, there are people who are starving and being ill-treated and persecuted. Now, so many years after our own experiences, we see a revival of Nazism and anti-Semitism, and our own memories of the not-so-distant past are cast into sharp relief. And all this in a day and age when we like to believe those spectres have been consigned to the past forever.

So long as there is even the slightest possibility of the cataclysmic events of history repeating themselves, I feel that we have a duty to bring our knowledge of that dark era into the uncompromising light of day. If once one has been trapped in a hell like Theresienstadt, one can never forget it.

Is it possible that such enormities could ever be perpetrated again?

Illustrations

In Theresienstadt, Leo Haas

In Theresienstadt, Leo Haas

Courtyard in K3 Theresienstadt, Leo Haas

The blind, Leo Haas

Corner of the room where the Danes were hurled together

Theresienstadt 1943, Jo Spier

The count-out outside Theresienstadt on 17 November 1943

Mass burial, Leo Haas

The daily ration

Bread is delivered, Malvina Schalková

Old prisoners delivered for transport

Last supper before the transport leaves, Jiři Valdštýn

Camp money

Transportation to the unknown

Camp money

Going to the transport, Helga Weissová-Hoškova

Going to the transport, Helga Weissová-Hoškova

Gate to the Gestapo prison at the small fortress, Theresienstadt, where the mayor, Mr Eppstein was put to death

Execution, Leo Haas

Execution, Leo Haas

Dwelling for the feeble minded, Bedřich Fritta

Morits and Mélanie Oppenhejm in Hitler's propaganda film about Theresienstadt

Queuing for soup

*Secret photograph of the gallows in Theresienstadt,
taken illegally by the Czech policeman Karel Salaber*

One transport arrives another leaves, Karel Fleischmann

The registration, Karel Fleischmann